D0447072

# ACKNOWLEDGMENTS

I wish to especially thank my daughter, Nancy Miller, vice-president and senior editor of Pocket Books and director of Washington Square Press, for her valuable editorial help and advice during the initial stages of this work. Thanks to Jim Booher, M.D., Sid Stubbs, Esq., Mark Band, CPA, and Irene Turton, R. N., for keeping my facts straight in the medical, legal, financial, and health-care aspects of life and to the Rev. Kerry Robb for his aid and support over the years. Many thanks to Jane Gurin for her helpful advice on communications and to Helen Sullivan for her savvy about people and what makes them tick. Undying thanks to Alex and Sharon Porven for rescuing me at all hours of the day and night from computer glitches. Grateful thanks to my longtime friend Pat Dalton for her support and encouragement, and to Lou Marcati and his gang who were there in my times of need. Many thanks to Benno Kling and Jim R. Asker for their generous help and thanks to Debra Ricci—keeper of the Zip drive. I also wish to acknowledge my indebtedness to the late Dr. Penelope Russianoff, from whom I learned so much on the topic of communication.

This book would not have been written without the bravery, courage, and grace I saw in the patients who came to me for help over the years. I am grateful for all that I've learned from them and they are the true inspiration for making *Plan B* known to a wider audience.

Many thanks also to my agent, Carla Glasser, and my editor, Sheila M. Curry, who helped make writing this book a most pleasant experience.

And last but not least, I am grateful to my husband, Jim, for his love, encouragement, suggestions, and general cheering-on, during the writing of this book and always.

# SAY YES TO A HAPPY, MEANINGFUL LIFE

You know all about Plan B—it's been your fallback position in everyday situations. But it's probably a new idea to think of Plan B as leading to permanent, satisfying solutions for the problems you face. Take the following quiz and discover your need to make a change.

1. Are you false in relationship to yourself, your partner, family, or job? Or are people false to you?

2. Do you ignore signals that something is wrong or "off" in the situations you're involved in?

3. Do you disregard facts that need facing and, instead, push them aside?

4. Are you unwilling to look at new ideas and believe that "this is the way things are"?

5. Are you unhappy in your life and do you feel you were born that way?

6. Do you believe you'll never achieve the goals you long for?

7. Do you feel you don't *deserve* to be happy?

8. Do you suspect there's something in your background that prevents you from reaching your full potential?

9. Do you go around in circles and never find a way out?

10. If your life ended now, would you regret what you've left undone?

The more times you respond with Yes to these questions, the more likely it is that you are living an inauthentic life—a life untrue to your self and your real goals and aims. The good news is that *Plan B* can help you get unstuck and get moving in another direction.

Most Perigee Books are available at special quantity discounts for bulk purchases for sales promotions, premiums, fund-raising or educational use. Special books, or book excerpts, can also be created to fit specific needs.

For details, write Special Markets, The Berkley Publishing Group, 375 Hudson Street, New York, New York 10014.

# Plan
# B

How to Get Unstuck
from Work, Family, and
Relationship Problems

STEPHANIE ASKER, LCSW

A Perigee Book

To That Wonderful Bunch of People—
My Family

A Perigee Book
Published by The Berkley Publishing Group
A division of Penguin Putnam Inc.
375 Hudson Street
New York, New York 10014

Copyright © 1999 by Stephanie Asker, LCSW
Book design by Tiffany Kukec
Interior author photograph by Kathryn Kennedy Photography
Cover design by Miguel Santana

All rights reserved. This book, or parts thereof,
may not be reproduced in any form without permission.

First edition: December 1999

Published simultaneously in Canada.

The Penguin Putnam Inc. World Wide Web site address is
http://www.penguinputnam.com

Library of Congress Cataloging-in-Publication Data

Asker, Stephanie.
    Plan B: how to get unstuck from work, family, and
relationship problems / Stephanie Asker.—1st ed.
        p.   cm.
    Includes bibliographical references and index.
    ISBN 0-399-52566-1 (trade paper)
    1. Problem solving. 2. Problem solving—Case studies. I. Title.
BF449 .A75 1999
158—dc21                                          99-046839
                                                        CIP

Printed in the United States of America

10  9  8  7  6  5  4  3  2  1

# CONTENTS

## Contents

# INTRODUCTION

We each have a gift to bring to the world. If we're successful, we'll fulfill ourselves and those around us and live in peace and joy. But many people are so burdened by unresolved problems that they never live out the lives for which they were created and meant to enjoy. This book is about finding *solutions* to problems—your problems—and learning a system that enables you to deal with whatever life throws your way—with boldness, confidence, and self-assurance.

As a psychotherapist and marriage counselor, it makes me happy to see someone who had arrived at my office dejected and despairing, leave some time later, glowing and vibrant. This familiar scenario made me wonder how I could help people *before* they came to see me—before they hit bottom.

After much trial and error, I came up with a method I felt was simple to understand and easy to follow. I wanted to help people look at their problems in a new way. I wanted them to realize that they weren't *stuck* in a bad situation but to recognize that situation as a signal to change, and to give them the tools to make those changes.

Most of us have areas in our lives that we're stuck in. Family members bicker for twenty years and will do so for twenty more. We're trapped in relationships that go nowhere, but can't walk away. Relationships with parents are full of guilt and pain that never get any better. We feel trapped in jobs we hate but somehow can't seem to leave.

My hope for you is that reading *Plan B* will help you identify the problem areas in your life, untangle yourself from the messes, and live out your hopes and dreams. Whether you suffer from a difficult family situation, low self-esteem, or destructive relationships, this book will help you become more authentically *you* so that your talents and gifts will shine forth and your life will have the purpose and meaning it was meant to have. My wish for you is that this book helps you get unstuck from problems that have plagued you for years, and shows you the path to the happiness and productivity that is rightfully yours.

In my practice over the last twenty-five years, I've seen much suffering—unhappy couples, abused spouses, depressed and anxious men and women, and people who don't know how to navigate their daily lives. They know they have problems. The trouble is they don't know there are solutions for them. While I rejoice in the successful work we do together to heal these emotional wounds, it hurts to see so much initial pain.

I began to notice a common thread among all of my patients. Whether they were individuals suffering from depression or a couple contemplating divorce, they came to me not to find a solution, but to find relief from their pain. It's very painful to walk around with chronic problems—as painful as a persistent toothache or a lingering headache. *Pain* is the thread that characterizes lives gone awry.

A good therapist listens carefully to the patient and elicits a detailed history about most of the problem areas in his or her life. Working on untangling these problems means working together on a plan that helps the patient choose the solution that works—a solution that eliminates or eases the pain. I discovered that there are three stages to almost any therapy:

- **Stage One** consists of exploring all aspects of a problem: the way it exists in reality, the emotional and psychological feelings you bring to the problem and the way you deal with it on a daily basis.

- **Stage Two** consists of helping you see alternatives to the way you've responded to problems in the past. This is a difficult task, since people usually feel so entrenched in their particular situation that they consider their way of life immutable, unopen to any change or modification, no matter how much they may ardently wish for it.

- **Stage Three** is the most exciting. You'll become able to see that change is possible and, hopefully, be eager to implement that change. As success breeds success, it becomes easier to reach the goal of a life transformed by choices that are correct for you and help you become a more loving, joyful person. In this stage, you'll learn to deal with problems in a solution-oriented manner. You'll become decisive and confident, putting behind forever the outworn, ineffective techniques that have kept you stuck and unable to achieve your goals.

We all begin life with rosy dreams for our future. Being popular in school, graduating at the top our class, finding a job where we're appreciated and fulfilled, getting married and having kids, owning a decent car and a nice house in a good neighborhood, and being surrounded by loving friends and family make up the good life we all hope for. When some of these dreams aren't fulfilled, most of us keep trying harder to achieve them. These dreams are what I call Plan A. *Plan A is the original scenario we created to allow us to acquire the physical, emotional, and financial goods we want in life.* We may have scripted Plan A in our preteen or adolescent years, but when our adult lives take un-scripted detours, as lives always do, the Plan A we've con-structed for ourselves doesn't necessarily work.

A classic example of this is Laura, a slim, blond 24-year-old administrative assistant, who came to me complaining of being fearful of leaving home and striking out on her own. Twice she had found a small, one-bedroom apart-ment, and twice, when it came time to sign the lease, she had backed out at the last minute. After two months in therapy, Laura realized that the cause of her problem was her unresolved relationship with her father. As a little girl, she naturally wanted her father to love her—that was Plan A. Yet in all the years she lived at home, her father had treated her with contempt and disdain and nothing Laura did or tried to do changed that scenario. Since Laura's Plan A was to have her father love her, unconsciously *she was going to stay at home until he did.* Once Laura understood that her father might never be capable of giving her what she deserved—a parent's love—she reluctantly abandoned Plan A. A few months later, she signed a lease on a small apartment and embarked on Plan B: looking for love with a partner who could love her in return. Two years later, Laura called and said she might need a larger apartment soon. She'd been seriously dating Tim, a young reporter who had just proposed to her, and they planned to get married in the spring.

If Laura hadn't discarded Plan A, she would not have been able to move on emotionally in her life. Abandoning Plan A enabled her to change her original goal (getting love from her father) and move toward a new goal (getting love from a husband). Most of the patients I see are stuck in some variation of this script. They hang on to hopes and dreams that can never be fulfilled and therefore never chase the dream that's awaiting them.

Like many of us, Laura's Plan B turned out to be much better than the Plan A she had clung to for so long. In school, A is the best grade and B is second best. But in life, Plan B often will get us to the personal, emotional, and financial goals we dream of after we've been stuck in a Plan A that's failed us. We choose Plan B when it's our *best* choice and Plan A is really no choice at all.

My job is to help patients learn when to persevere in pursuing Plan A and when to give up. It's to help them learn how to investigate alternatives and see their choices clearly. Knowing when to walk away from something is one of the most difficult decisions we're ever called upon to make. The problem is that we often don't realize we *have* a choice. Once we realize that choices are available and that there are systematic steps to help choose the best one, then finding Plan B becomes an easy habit rather than an inconceivable idea. This book is about helping you so that you can learn how to avoid the traps and snares you've chosen in the past and go on to a brighter, happier future.

Chapter Two will help you differentiate between a Plan A that's worth pursuing and one that needs to be scrapped. We all cheer the Olympic athlete who has a stress fracture, yet runs the race and wins the gold. You and I might never think of continuing, but the athlete does, and pursues Plan A despite all odds. Is your Plan A worth gritting your teeth and suffering for, or will it never lead to the gold? If you decide that Plan A will keep you running the race, exhausted yet never winning, you're ready for Plan B.

Plan B is the *solution* you choose to attain the life you opt for—the loving spouse, the satisfying career, the centeredness and peace of mind that comes from fulfilling your talents, gifts, and ability to love, undistracted by anger, fear, and depression. The new path you choose to reach these goals may be a detour, a total abandonment of the original plan, or a new passage. Any one of these choices may be valid depending upon your temperament and circumstances. Chapters Three and Four will teach you how to search for, choose, and implement the plan that's right for you.

*Plan B* will teach you how to find your true path and your true self. When you find one, you find the other. Too many of us live our lives in a joyless, constricted manner. "Is that all there is?" is a question too many of us ask too much of the time. This book will help you look at your life in a new way and find solutions to your most pressing problems.

# First, Look at Your Problems

No one gets through life unscathed. The longer we live, the greater the opportunity for problems to accumulate, like barnacles, on the surface of the lives we lead. By the time we reach adulthood, this accumulation interferes with the steady progress we've come to expect as we reach toward our goals.

This book is written to help beleaguered people everywhere find a system for solutions to the problems that plague them and prevent them from living a joyous life. As a psychotherapist and marriage counselor, I've come to see that patients aren't aware of solutions for their problems—their only "solution" is to keep trying to achieve an unworkable Plan A. They come seeking relief from the pain, *without realizing that pain goes away when solutions are found.* One of the main reasons we get stuck in the same merry-go-round of conflict and chaos is that, though our pain hurts, we don't know what the cure is. Psychotherapy and marriage counseling help by offering permanent solutions to long-standing problems—they help people change their Plan A or find a better Plan B.

Learning how to modify Plan A when it no longer works, or how to abandon it and choose the correct Plan B, may avoid the need for psychotherapy or marriage counseling entirely. Learning to recognize emotional pain as a signal to seek satisfactory solutions and discovering how to implement those solutions is exactly how good counseling and therapy work. In these days of managed care, where office visits are strictly limited, it's more essential than ever to be able to deal with and resolve the problems life scatters along our path.

Problems cause us to have both too much and too little energy. We use too much energy by forcing down the lid on the pressure cooker of our anxiety, depression, and rage. With too little energy, we live our lives on empty. The fuel is our physical, emotional, and psychic energy and our journey is affected when we're running on a low tank. Our fuel is drained by our anger and coping mechanisms, with nothing left over for living. If you've ever been obsessed by a broken love affair or are going home tonight to an alcoholic spouse, you'll probably agree that 75 percent of your energy is burned up by your problem.

Look at the following illustration:

Seventy-five percent of the first chart is taken up by the problem, and only 25 percent is available to you for life. Now, look at the second chart and think what you might

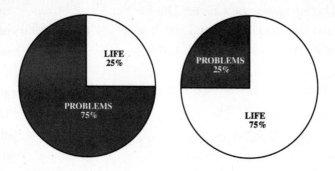

do with triple the energy you have inside of you if it weren't being diverted on a daily basis.

How can we learn to use that newly available energy and find a pathway out of our troubles? A method that's simple and logical and that *works* is called the Solution-Oriented Life. There are three steps to the Solution-Oriented Life:

**Step One:** Realize you *have* a problem.

**Step Two:** Think in terms of a *solution* to your problem.

**Step Three:** Find the correct solution for *you*.

## STEP ONE: REALIZE YOU HAVE A PROBLEM

How enmeshed are you in life's problems? How side-tracked are you from the direction you're meant to take? How do you know whether your Plan A is working or it's time to move on to Plan B?

**Are You Living the Correct Life for You?**
Take the quiz below and see how many of the following questions you answer with a yes:

_____  1.  Do you feel centered, no matter how difficult your life?

_____  2.  Do you feel off balance or manipulated in relationships?

_____  3.  Do you feel content or enthusiastic about life?

_____  4.  Do you feel depressed or moody much of the time?

_____  5.  Do you feel angry or irritable at those around you?

_____  6.  Do you feel anxious or worried in your daily life?

_____  7.  Do you have low energy without a physical cause?

_____  8.  Do you eat, smoke, or drink too much, or are you addicted in other ways?

_____  9.  Do you expend much energy to accomplish very little?

_____ 10.  Do you feel out of control of your life?

If you answered yes to question 1, you're probably living the correct life for you *at the present time*. You may have been laid off from your job, or perhaps you are taking care of a sick relative, and this isn't how you want life to continue. But your priorities and values are in synch with your circumstances, and you have the confidence and inner strength that you'll prevail.

If you answered yes to question 3, either your Plan A is working or you've learned how to search for and implement the Plan B that's correct for you. You may be one of the lucky few where everything you touch turns to the gold of happiness, but more likely you've learned to be flexible and reflective about your life. Contentment and enthusiasm are wonderful traits and they're a touchstone for you to tell whether you're on track in your life.

But if you answered yes to any of the other eight questions, you're suffering pain, and the pain is multiplied by the number of yes answers you gave. If you answered yes only to being irritable or being worried, you didn't score 90 percent. That irritability or that worry permeates your life, saps your energy, and *is caused by an unresolved problem*. And most likely, you've checked off more than one, since unresolved problems tend to multiply.

If you answered no to question 1 or 3, or yes to any of the others, something is going on in your life that needs addressing. Step One should help you see whether you have a problem and realize that a way exists for you to minimize or eliminate it. Changing your Plan A or finding a good Plan B is the key to the Solution-Oriented Life; later chapters will teach you how to find specific solutions for your particular problems.

It seems absurd that most people suffer day in and day

out from abuse, marital conflict, depression, fear, anger, and a host of other difficulties, *yet do not realize they have a problem*. What they realize is that they're hurting or enraged or bitchy or suicidal. But they accept that as the way they were born, or the way life is. Therefore, they do nothing except endure another day of anguish.

Many people who've grown up in a dysfunctional family don't know what normal is. They have no touchstone as to feelings of centeredness, stability, or honesty in relationships. They can't assess life realistically. When they scream at each other as their parents did, it's normal. When they're constantly irritable or depressed, they're just bitchy or have a temper. When they're consumed by anxiety, it's normal, especially when, say, their mother was anxious about driving or traveling far from home. If Plan A is the life of peace, fulfillment, and good relationships, they're living Plan A gone awry.

The following story will illustrate how an inability to see a needed change from Plan A to a good Plan B kept Kristin stuck in the chronic pain of a hurtful relationship. (All case histories and examples in this book are true, though identifying details have been changed to protect people's privacy).

Kristin was a quiet, single woman in her early 20s, working as a secretary in a brokerage house. She'd been having an affair with her boss, Neil, for the past year and had been unhappy in the relationship most of that time. Neil was married and though he and Kristin really loved each other, Neil couldn't bring himself to divorce his wife and leave their two children. But he also couldn't bring himself to give up Kristin. Neil was stuck, and therefore Kristin felt stuck too.

Kristin's Plan A was to be with Neil in a permanent relationship. When he found himself unable to get a divorce and make a wholehearted commitment to her, Kristin couldn't find a way out of the messy situation. She hadn't formulated a workable Plan A. The Plan A she'd devised was, "Neil is the man I need to be with for the rest of my life." No wonder she felt at a loss when he wouldn't get a divorce and marry her. Kristin at first tried to modify her Plan A by asking Neil to go into counseling, but when he refused, she felt rejected and betrayed. She finally entered therapy, as so many people do, when her plan had reached the meltdown stage.

Like all of us, Kristin wanted to keep her Plan A. She felt stuck for many sessions, since she perceived that giving up her plan meant giving up having a boyfriend now or in the future. After careful work in therapy, she realized that because her mother had tolerated the many affairs her father had had throughout their marriage, Kristin had formulated her Plan A based on her mother's behavior—salvation lay with a particular man and that man only. When that man was unable to be a true companion and satisfy her healthy need for an exclusive relationship, Kristin's life could only remain a depressing and miserable affair.

Five months after Kristin realized that she could choose a happier life than that of her parents, Kristin announced she was leaving Neil. She had become emotionally strong enough to give up Plan A to have Neil as a lover and, with help, formulated Plan B—"a boyfriend I'll be happy with and who's free to be with me." Giving up Plan A meant realizing that Neil would never leave his wife and children.

Neil was not Kristin's problem. There are many bosses like Neil, married people willing to have affairs with their unmarried assistants, but single employees don't have to choose them as their lovers. Kristin's problem lay within herself, in her formulating a Plan A that allowed only Neil to be her partner, and believing life without him would be too isolated and lonely. If Kristin had realized *she* had the problem, her next thought might have been, "What can I do about it?" But until she realized a problem existed *within herself,* she couldn't make that observation.

If you feel stuck, you have a *problem* you are stuck in; if you recognize you need solutions, you need solutions to the *problems* you have. When you have a problem and don't admit it, you're in denial and lying to yourself. Lying to yourself is the most harmful thing you can do. Better to say, "I've got a drinking problem, but I won't deal with it now." Or, "He's emotionally abusive but I don't want to be lonely, so I'm afraid to leave." What these honest statements enable you to do *is to stop feeling crazy* when you tell the truth to yourself, because then your inner knowledge will match the outer reality you see around you. You feel crazy when you have problems that you refuse to recognize, or worse, when you tell yourself that your problems are no problem at all—"My drinking isn't a problem," or, "He'll leave his wife soon and we'll be happy."

The most important thing I teach my patients is that it's *safe* to discover what their options are and then not do a thing about them *unless and until they're ready to do so.* For example, a gay person may be terrified of coming out but realize that living a lie is crippling him emotionally. It's important for him to understand that he can tell people the truth about himself *next week, next month, next year, or never.* This principle is one of the most liberating though seemingly simple ideas people can learn; it frees them to explore every aspect of their lives and to find the Plan B that's right for them.

Fear is what usually prevents you from pursuing healthy change: fear of the unknown, fear of becoming a healthy person and being introduced to someone you may not know—yourself. There's truth to the old saw, "The devil you know is better than the devil you don't know." But keeping up the pretense can be too much hard work, and you may eventually crumble under it.

For instance, if your matrimonial Plan A has gone awry and you're stuck in an unhappy marriage, many paths are available to you; divorce is only one of them. People are afraid to examine a bad marriage because they think the next step is running to an attorney and starting divorce proceedings. Nothing could be further from the truth. Other alternatives might be more helpful. One is to enter marriage counseling, which I recommend for many reasons. I've seen miracles happen with couples who didn't seem to stand a chance in the world. You could discover you do want a divorce, but it would be easier when the kids aren't 2, 4, and 7 and you have no job skills. Counseling can teach you how to separate without enormous anger. Older couples might decide to stay together because their lives are so intertwined with family and finances that they are better off coexisting by following different interests and taking separate vacations. You could resolve to stay married despite the fact that what's wrong can never be fixed because you've been taught divorce is a sin. Choosing your Plan B is up to you. And *when* to implement that plan is also your decision. *No one is going to make you do anything.* But you'll feel like a centered, sane human being if you do decide to take time and wait until you're ready.

People fear initiating change because they look too far into the future and it scares them to death. They imagine that Step One leads all the way to Step Twenty-five, but *Step One leads only to Step Two, if and when you decide to take it.* If an abused wife attends a battered women's group, she need never attend another one. Only if she feels it helped and looks forward to another meeting does she need ever go again. And she's *never* compelled to go beyond that point. Step Two might consist of reading books about battered wives. Step Three could involve seeing a counselor. Step Eighteen might be actually leaving her abusive husband—but she needn't do so *unless and until* she's resolved all fears and practical issues. Realizing this removes much of the panic we feel when facing new lives and new challenges. You may still experience some fear, *but you won't have to feel crazy.*

The freedom this concept brings can set you free from your anxieties and constitutes one of the real breakthroughs in psychotherapy and marriage counseling. Understanding that problem solving is a process and that processes take time enables you to relax and proceed on your own timetable. But that's not an excuse for no progress at all. Taking steps in small doses that you're comfortable with is the key to moving forward and to increasing self-esteem. There is much truth in the old Chinese proverb, "The journey of a thousand miles begins with but a single step."

Taking these steps will begin to enlarge the Life area on your chart and increase the emotional energy available to you. You'll be examining Plan A and admitting that your rosy dream has become drab and tattered. While this will (and *ought*) to make you sad, it's the first, necessary step toward removing the debris from your relationships and your life and beginning to realize your dreams.

## STEP TWO: THINK IN TERMS OF A SOLUTION TO YOUR PROBLEM

Once you can safely admit to yourself you have a problem, you're free to think an entirely new thought: "What's the Solution?" Now that you can entertain options without jumping into action, you're free to take weeks, months, and even years to arrive at problem-solving solutions. Most people never think in terms of solutions. How many relationships would be both pleasant and *fun* if solutions could be found for all the big and little problems as they arise?

Donna and George, a couple in their mid-30s, lived with their two preschool children in a large apartment on the Upper West Side of Manhattan. It's a neighborhood near museums, Lincoln Center, and the other cultural advantages of New York City. Though George is an attorney and Donna a guidance counselor, their combined salaries were stretched to the limit in order to pay for their expensive condo and day care for Michael, 4, and Tracy, 2. Their

Plan A was to raise their family in the city so they could be close to the children while at work and take advantage of all the cultural benefits they so enjoyed. But what was looming on the horizon was the cost of tuition for two at a good private school, since the public schools were not up to their standards. When they looked at their budget, they recognized that the tuition fees would leave them struggling in an unacceptable way.

At first, it was impossible for them to face giving up their dream—staying in New York in an apartment they loved. But they realized that unless they won the lottery or received an inheritance from a rich uncle—who didn't exist—the financial stress would be unbearable, and a new solution was imperative. Once they began to entertain a new plan—Plan B—the solution to their problem gradually became clear. One year later, they chose to move to Hastings, a suburb in Westchester County, New York, where there are excellent public schools and many other professional families (some of whom they knew and had preceded them in their move from the city). The money they saved from private-school fees were spent instead on reducing a mortgage. New York was a short train ride away and they continued to take the children to the Museum of Natural History, the zoo, and *The Nutcracker*. But, best of all, they had a fenced-in yard and Michael and Tracy could play with their new friends unattended, a situation impossible in the city. When Donna and George had settled into their new home, they realized how stuck they would have been if they had remained in New York and how thinking of a new plan—a *solution* to their predicament—helped them live a better dream instead of a financial nightmare.

Donna and George's example shows how thinking in terms of a solution to your problem not only helps with the problem itself, but other problems you may not even have been aware of. For instance, it was a matter of course for them or the nanny to be with the children every moment they were outside while they lived in Manhattan. It was only after they had a fenced-in yard, and the neighbors did too, that they saw how much easier it was to keep an eye on the kids from a kitchen window and how they had probably gained an hour a day of time in which to catch up on their household chores.

Small problems are also solved by thinking in terms of solutions to them. For example, Julie was disgusted with John for leaving his socks and underwear on the bedroom floor. Lack of communication was the problem here; she assumed both their Plan A's were "We'll each clean up after ourselves," but John's Plan A was "Julie will clean up after me just as my mother did." Every time she saw his laundry on the carpet she became enraged, and her anger and bitterness kept her at the boiling point much of the time. The problem was that Julie didn't want to pick up John's clothes, and John "forgot" to pick up after himself because underwear on the floor wasn't his job.

The solution they found was something both partners could agree to and seemed fair to both sides. Julie bought an attractive basket and placed it at John's side of the bed. John still dropped his clothes where he stood, but now he dropped them into the basket and not on the floor. When this solution worked, one more item was ticked off the list of their complaints. Each solution they found to a seemingly small problem gave them hope for their future happiness. When they learned to compare Plan A's to see whether they were in agreement, and to compromise if they were not, they gained a feeling of confidence that they'd resolve the other issues that were coming between them.

Another example of the stress reduction that results from problem solving is the story of Sharon and Ed. They had happily led an upscale lifestyle until Ed was injured in an auto accident and had to go on disability. Sharon had a high-paying, high-stress job as the comptroller of a mid-sized corporation, so income wasn't a problem. Instead, because of Ed's injuries, the division of labor fell disproportionately on her, and Ed felt inadequate because he couldn't do all that was needed. When they had a baby, Sharon's stress level rose to the danger point and their marriage was in serious trouble.

After three months of marriage counseling, Ed, Sharon, and their baby, Tommy, took a vacation at a beach house at a remote spot on the North Carolina coast. They came back aglow and not just from the vacation. They had continued to discuss various solutions to their problem and realized that the lifestyle they had constructed when Ed was healthy had become too much of a burden. They decided they wanted to live a less complicated life. Though they had come to no definite decisions as to how to go about this, they were excited about considering such options as (1) a less stressful job for Sharon (2) moving to a rural area and managing on Ed's disability income, or (3) moving to

Mexico or Costa Rica where his disability income would not only pay for household expenses but a nanny and housekeeper as well. Even though they felt they couldn't make a change for a year because of Sharon's commitment to a work project, the fact that they knew they *would* alter their lifestyle immediately relieved the pressure on both of them. Not only that, but the thrill of fantasizing about their future, which now consisted of a joint vision, healed the antagonism they felt when too many of the marital chores fell on Sharon's shoulders alone.

In all of these examples, sticking with the original Plan A was *causing* the problem. Only by modifying Plan A or finding Plan B were these couples able to find less stress and more peace and satisfaction in their lives. Donna and George found themselves with a better dream than the one they had thought was ideal. Julie and John gave themselves hope by finding a new solution to a seemingly small problem. Sharon and Ed restored a loving relationship by revising their goals and exchanging the materialism that had become a burden for a simpler life. These examples show that allowing yourself to realize there's a problem, then permitting yourself to think in terms of a solution to that problem, not only can enlarge your world but can also lower your stress level and improve your relationships. It doesn't matter whether your problem is as small as underwear on the floor or as large as changing your entire life. Once you let yourself entertain options and envision solutions to your problems, you can begin to climb out of the quicksand you feel mired in and find new happiness and direction for your life.

## Step Three: Find the Correct Solution for *You*

Finding a solution is difficult and can take a few weeks or many months. It's important not to be hasty and choose an option too quickly—that's jumping from the frying pan into the fire. Chapters Three, Four, and Five will help you plan methodically, and step by step, how to choose a solution that's correct for you, no matter what your problem.

We all know people who hate the circumstances they find themselves in and impulsively choose a way out. There's the woman with three or four marriages, the worker who moves from job to job, or the man who ricochets from relationship to relationship. Trying more of the same doesn't help. It isn't the marriage, the job, or the relationship that's at fault in these instances. It's most likely an unresolved problem within that causes these people to keep embracing inappropriate choices. Chapter Five will look at the way in which you may be sabotaging yourself, and methods to avoid repeating these errors.

How do you find the *correct* solution for your particular problem? Let's look at the story of Tina and see how she arrived at the solution that fit her needs:

Tina was a single, 25-year-old working woman who came to me for treatment of low-level depression. She was unhappy living in Maryland, since all her friends and family were back in Michigan. She had come to Baltimore to go to school and become a paralegal, and had stayed on when she received an attractive offer from a prestigious law firm. She owned a small townhouse and had an outwardly pleasant life. The only trouble was, it wasn't the life she wanted.

When she spoke of her present existence, her longing for home became apparent. She had never faced this yearning because she was afraid to uproot her life. She knew what the problem was—she missed her friends, parents, cousins, and siblings. But she felt stuck in Baltimore because the possibility of a solution never crossed her mind. She was afraid to think of moving and selling her townhouse, because the real-estate market was depressed. She was terrified to consider leaving her job because what if she couldn't find as good a one back home? Instead, she cried after phone calls from her mother and endlessly reread letters from her best friend. *Fear* kept her from considering her options, and it took some time to reassure her that it was safe to at least contemplate returning home.

As soon as Tina learned that having a problem meant thinking about the answer to the question, "What's the Solution?" she was able to admit, over a period of months, that her heart was back in the Midwest and she wanted to follow her heart. Once she examined her choices, it took her three months to decide to return home. She sold her townhouse at a slight loss, but her severance pay covered her moving expenses. Since that time, Tina has moved to a small house in a suburb near the city where she grew up. And she's earning the same salary she did in Baltimore, in an area with a lower cost of living. Today, she's very happy she made the move.

You can test whether a solution is the correct one for you by asking the following questions: Will it work? Does it make you feel enthusiastic instead of depleted? If the answer to both of these questions is yes, then it's probably a solution that's correct for you.


Paul arrived in my office in a sorry state. Though not usually a heavy drinker, he had been abusing alcohol the last few months in an effort to escape his unhappy professional life. He loved his wife, Suzy, and he loved his children, but he hated his job and couldn't deal with the role reversal his wife's inheritance had caused. Brought up to believe that the man supplies the bulk of the income, he had lost his self-esteem when his father-in-law died and left Suzy a large fortune. It was so much money they couldn't ignore it, and though Suzy was unassuming, her money was *there*. Yet Paul's self-worth was tied into his role as husband, working in a productive, achieving job. The only way Paul knew how to counteract his terrible feelings was to work harder at his job and try to rise ever higher on the corporate ladder.

The trouble was that his corporation, like most, had downsized and the employees, especially the executives, were expected to work long hours, including nights and weekends. In addition, the company had diversified into areas that didn't appeal to Paul and he was put in charge of one of those very divisions. Paul would never have been happy with this state of affairs, but it seemed especially ludicrous in light of the fact that he didn't need to work at all. He knew he needed to find a solution, but couldn't think of one that was correct for his particular situation.

Paul understood that the only option he had entertained—working harder at his job—was ruining his well-being, his emotional health, and his marriage. So, the first thing we worked on was helping him recognize that he needed to enlarge his repertoire of choices in order to develop a viable Plan B. It was wonderful to see first his relief and later his enthusiasm when plan after plan was discussed and put in the "yes," "no" or "maybe" column.

Four months later, a plan emerged with which Paul felt genuinely happy. He discussed it with Suzy and their vote was, "Go for it." Paul gave a month's notice and resigned from the company. He opened his own consulting firm, specializing in the areas that pleased him. They agreed to splurge (something difficult for him) on furnishing the office, and Suzy took on the job of decorating it, selecting dark paneling, tasteful fabrics, and good furniture throughout. But the heart of the plan was to work only 50 percent of the time on consulting and use the remaining 50 percent doing something very necessary—managing the fortune Suzy had inherited.

The reason this solution was the correct one for Paul (and Suzy too) was that the money really did need managing, but Suzy had absolutely no interest in doing so. Paul was still able to do important work in his field, for which he was highly paid, but he was also able to use his financial skills to oversee the inheritance. He derived great pride in seeing what a good job he was doing in making the money grow. His self-esteem was high, his hours were shorter, his alcohol abuse ended, and the job pressure evaporated. He loved his new life and he and Suzy were thrilled with the solution.

A happy side effect of choosing the correct solution for

ourselves is that since the solution is correct, *the consequences of those solutions are also correct.*

When Tina returned to Michigan, she felt more at peace than she ever had. Her depression disappeared because she was living the life she wanted—among family and friends who loved and supported her. She had more energy available for her job and received two promotions within eighteen months. And she could finally afford the single-family home she had only been able to dream about back in Maryland.

Paul, too, found himself doing what he was ideally suited for: working without pressure in the field he was trained in, balanced with his new interest—overseeing an inheritance he could now feel was also his, since he was investing his time and expertise in managing it on a daily basis. The bonus was that Suzy had so much fun decorating Paul's office that she decided to leave her retailing job and return to school to study interior design, which she felt was more creative.

There are solutions that will enable you to live life to the fullest—and experiencing life to the fullest has different meanings at differing times of life. Time and circumstances change Plan A. A single person at age 25 may enjoy traveling to foreign destinations, but if that same person at age 35 has a family, money may need to be spent instead on day care and clothes for the kids. Changing Plan A from exotic travel to mundane expenses doesn't diminish Plan A at all—indeed, it may enhance it—as long as you're living the life that fulfills your needs, interests, and values. You experience problems only when the difficulties of life are not met with creative solutions.

Unfortunately, you may also create problems for yourself by not recognizing that time has changed your life and you need to find different solutions for differing needs. If you continue to spend as much money on entertainment when you have children as you did when you were single, you'll probably find yourself in financial difficulty. You need to find a new plan that will take into account a larger home and children's needs. If you're a woman who's decided in the past to stay at home and raise your children and now they're in school all day, you may want to revise your plan in order to find new structure and purpose in your daily life.

Many people are unhappy because they don't realize that a Plan A that was valid ten years ago needs revising to fit today's needs—and will continue to need revising periodically throughout life. The best way to deal with this is to regularly update a "problem list" and see what difficulties you're experiencing in all the areas of your daily life. See whether you're unhappy with a close relationship or feeling stuck in a job that's going nowhere. Then consider whether your Plan A has been outgrown and needs modification, or should be scrapped altogether and replaced with a good Plan B. This can be an exciting and rewarding task, one that can make your life work for you in the very best way possible. And doing so can also eliminate problems that weren't really problems at all—merely the natural rhythm and flow of life as it continues to unfold.

# FINDING A SOLUTION:
## Your Plan A—Reality or Fantasy?

We all begin our lives with hopes and dreams that constitute our Plan A. For most of us, Plan A consists of getting through school with good grades and good friends; graduating; finding an interesting, well-paying job; marrying; having kids; and living in a nice home and neighborhood. We visualize a problem-free life—no illness, no divorce, no alcoholism, no earthquakes (literal or figurative). But no one lives a life without detours and even a few derailments.

We all learned the proverb, "If at first you don't succeed, try, try again," in grade school; it's a useful guideline for achieving your goals. Most of us know someone who married and divorced twice, and found the love of their life on the third try. Or someone else who failed at three businesses, started a fourth and became very successful. Or a high school kid who was on the B team in baseball and finally made the A team in his senior year. They all profited by taking this concept to heart and steering their life by it.

So how can you tell whether you should continue to persevere in *your* Plan A? How can you tell whether you're going round and round on the same old treadmill or life is about to spin you off onto a new path?

If only we could peer into the future—but alas, we can't. Instead, we need to find other ways to assess our chances and make more satisfying choices for the future. This chapter will teach you how to differentiate the Plan A of your dreams from the nightmares of your existence. It will help you discover whether you can reach your goal by staying on your original course or whether you'll have to arrive at it by an entirely new path. Changing Plan A is making a detour to reach the *same* goal, while creating Plan B is defining a *new* one—for instance, the man who gives up his Plan A of "playing the field" in order to live his Plan B of achieving a mutually loving, enduring relationship.

*Plan A is the script we write in our early years that we feel will ensure our happiness.* It's our mission statement about who we want to be and how we want to live our lives, including lifestyle, employment, and relationships. At first our script consists of a broad dream; for many of us, it's a loving partner, a good job, and a nice home and family. As we grow older, it gets narrower and more specific—*this* partner, *this* career, *this* lifestyle, in this particular neighborhood.

By the time they have reached their 20s or 30s, most people have acquired some of these specific things or are on their way to getting them. Yet others have been disappointed in at least some of the choices they thought would fulfill their most cherished dreams. If you have been disappointed, it may be that your Plan A might not be your own, but that of your parents' dreams passed on to you. Or you or your parents may have envisioned a script of unrealistic expectations for you—becoming the President of the United States, for example—where you only have one chance in 250 million to succeed and none if you don't possess the required drive, talent, luck, and connections.

If your parents have imbued their script for your life into a plan you thought was your own, your plan may not feel right, but you may not understand why. Or if you admire your parents a great deal and consciously try to copy their goals, you need to take time to rethink them and decide whether these goals suit *you*. As a unique human being, your plan must fit your *own* talents and desires, not others'. Once you rethink goals, you're free to keep what you like and throw away the rest.

Another pattern that I see over and over again in therapy sessions is that patients may be consciously or unconsciously rebelling against their parents and purposely living a life opposite to the path their parents chose. You're not free if you live a life that's not your own but an imitation of someone else's. You're also not free if you must live your life *in opposition to* someone else's life or principles. The only way you can be free is if you pay attention to your own hopes, desires, dreams, and talents and choose a plan that fits those needs.

You need to examine your hopes and dreams and look to see whether they're really your own. If you suspect you're in the wrong job or the wrong relationship because you wanted to satisfy your parents, or you're tired of being a loser but you are one only because your family were such overachievers, rethink your script and try to write one that is made from choice, not conflict. You may need the help of a trusted friend or counselor in order to do this.

Once you have a Plan A, it basically consists of one of four variations:

1. *The Unsullied Dream:* All areas of your life match the dream you scripted in your youth. You're on track and on course.

2. *The Modified Dream:* Changing age and circumstances means Plan A probably needs some alterations. Change such as becoming a parent or moving far from home, as well as choosing partners and careers that aren't clones of your dreams, means matching a new script with your old Plan A in a way that will make you satisfied with the results.

3. *The Broken Dream:* Life has disappointed you in some or all major aspects of your existence. The possibility of changing Plan A within the old framework (same husband, same wife, same career) needs to be explored so you can decide whether Plan A is at all salvageable.

4. *Meltdown:* Plan A has totally broken down, but you may not recognize it as the cause of your personal nuclear wasteland of depression, rage, and despair.

This chapter will teach you how to differentiate Meltdown from Modified or Broken Dreams so you can decide whether Plan A will ever work for you or you need to concede failure and turn to a new option—Plan B.

## THE SATISFACTION SCALE

The following quiz will help you think about and assess where you are in your life. It will guide you to see where the dissatisfaction you feel is coming from. It will help you identify problems you need assistance with and give you a sense of satisfaction in recognizing areas where you really are living out your dreams. Answer each question with Always, Sometimes, Almost Never, or Never:

_____ 1. Are you content when alone, and do you value spending time with yourself?

_____ 2. Do you basically like yourself and what you stand for?

_____ 3. Are you now in, or have you had in the past, a fulfilling, intimate relationship?

_____ 4. Do you have supportive friends that you enjoy and that share your interests?

_____ 5. Do you look forward to being with relatives and do you (and your spouse and children, if any) have fun when together with them?

_____ 6. Do you have addicted, neurotic, or manipulative family members whom you allow to entrap you into repeated, nonproductive scenarios?

_____ 7. Are you on the road to a satisfying place in your work life?

_____ 8. Are you under too much pressure at work, without a way to reduce the stress?

_____ 9. Do you have a plan to accomplish the goals you've set for yourself in life—personal, family, spiritual, and financial? Are you on your way to achieving them and are you satisfied with your progress?

_____ 10. Are you involved in groups, charitable activities, or causes that help you feel you're making a difference to the world you live in?

Questions 1 and 2 relate to Self; 3 and 4 to Relationships; 5 and 6 to Family; 7 and 8 to Work; and 9 and 10 to Lifestyle. Except for questions 6 and 8, where the responses are reversed, the more Always and Sometimes responses you have, the higher you'll rate on the Satisfaction Scale. And, except for those two questions, the more Never and Almost Never responses, the higher the probability that you're experiencing difficulties in your daily life. As you examine your answers, you'll clearly see which aspects of your life you need to concentrate on most and which areas are relatively free of problems. *We're all aiming for a problem-free life, though we may never achieve it.* Remember, even if you have difficulty in only one area—whether it's Self, Relationships, Family, Work, or Lifestyle—it can spill over into other areas and infect every aspect of your existence.

For instance, if a work issue is depressing you, when you come home at night your depression and irritability may spill onto yourself, your partner, the kids, and even the dog. The corollary of this is that when you find solutions for this *one* area, the good feelings that result can also spread and affect you and those around you. When you take that first step and find a solution to your work problem, not only does your depression begin to lift, but the success you experience will give you confidence to begin to master other difficult areas in your life.

Six months after reading this book, it would be interesting to retake this quiz in light of the solutions you'll have devised for each sector. Hopefully, most of your answers will change in a more satisfactory direction and you will see your way clear to forever leave behind your Broken Dreams and Meltdowns.

As you read the rest of Chapter Two, decide whether you need to start big or start small. Some people are so upset by their biggest problem that they know they must begin to work on it right away *and feel ready to do so.* Don't begin by tackling your largest problem unless you know you're ready, or you'll have one more failure to berate yourself with. If you *do* decide to tackle a large problem (such as alcohol or drug addiction), don't sabotage yourself by trying to give up another large addiction (such as smoking) at the same time. *No matter how large or how many your problems, tackle one area at a time and don't move on to other areas until you've been successful in the original one.* If you tackle too many problems at once, you'll feel overwhelmed, defeated, and even more like a failure.

A benefit of overcoming *small* family problems, or making *little* changes in your work life, is that you'll experience success both in problem solving and in life in general. Success breeds success, and eventually by resolving many small problems, you'll get in the *habit* of success as well as finding your total life circumstances much improved. But whether you choose to face your largest or your smallest problem, it's *your* choice whether to work on a Modified or a Broken Dream first and *your* choice to know when you're really prepared to look Meltdown squarely in the face.

We live in a throwaway culture. So, when the specific spouse, career, or family relationship doesn't match up with an original dream—an original Plan A—it's easy to feel we should chuck the whole plan rather than concentrate on restoring our rosy vision. When our view of *ourselves* falls short of the dream, we may be tempted to blot out the discrepancy with an addiction—whether it be alcohol, drugs, food, shopping, sex, or workaholism—or give up and abandon our dreams altogether. We must realize that there is always another option—Plan B. We don't have to abandon everything, but if giving up on Plan A is our best choice, then we always have Plan B. Remember, *Plan B is very important, but it's to be used only when Plan A cannot be restored.*

In Kristin and Neil's situation, Kristin's original Plan A was to have a mutually loving, permanent relationship. But later, after they began their liaison, she became more focused and specific in her plan. Then her dream lover became the particular man, Neil. And when Neil couldn't satisfy her *narrower* plan, she thought she'd have to give up her dream altogether. When she learned to see that Plan A exists in four different versions, then she could begin to see into which category her affair fell.

Kristin's problem was either a Broken Dream or a Meltdown. Neil *had* no problem. His affair with Kristin was his Unsullied Dream. He had two women to love—his wife and Kristin—and two women who loved him. He lived in an intact home with his family, had a large social circle he enjoyed, and spent holidays taking trips and visiting relatives with his wife and children. Kristin realized that though she and Neil shared the same relationship, *she* was the only one with a plan that didn't match her dreams. She had no one to come home to; she had no one with whom to share her day, except in snatched conversations with Neil; and she was always alone on weekends and holidays.

Once she was able to realize that, for her, the affair represented either a Broken Dream or a complete Meltdown, she concentrated on one last try to restore the broken relationship. She gave herself a time limit of three months for herself and Neil to arrive at a conclusion that would satisfy both their dreams. But since Neil was satisfied with his plan, and *her* plan for him to divorce his wife and marry her would cause *him* grief, no progress was possible. It was clear that Kristin's plan was in Meltdown.

When your Plan A doesn't match your partner's, and neither one of you is willing or able to modify your plan so that each receives what you need, *your joint Plan A (to be happy together) is in Meltdown.* When that happens, both partners will be unhappy—Kristin had been upset for a long time, but Neil too was unable to be happy, since every time he was with Kristin, he saw and felt her depression and despair. *This is the essence of what goes wrong in unhappy marriages and affairs—Plan A's don't (and can't) match, so they become unbalanced, go downhill, and unravel.*

It's very important, when your plan doesn't match another's, to give the impasse time to work itself out. One reason is that both of you may have new thoughts and ideas when faced with the crisis of parting. You may try harder to fix the relationship and create new and shared goals. But the most important reason is that even though you know you must eventually part, very few people are able to say goodbye easily. Life and feelings are a process, and it takes most of us time to prepare ourselves to give up someone or something we love. In Kristin's case it was a love affair, but it's just as difficult to give up a job that once defined you and no longer does, or an alcoholic parent who is drunk and abusive every time you visit and refuses to acknowledge that a problem exists.

I see many people who give themselves a time limit for a situation to resolve, and then set it again and again. They go on and on living a life that's broken at best, and may actually be totally shattered. They have no new plan for their life—no Plan B. The good news is that almost all of them eventually feel they've hit a deadline and move on with their lives. Fortunately, when they *are* ready to move on, their words, deeds, and attitude show their spouse, boss, relative, or friend that they mean business—and that often inspires partners or colleagues to finally work together to fix the broken dream. *Deciding to change and acting that way is the best hope you have of making the other person in the relationship decide that he or she wants to continue with you in their lives in a new and healthier way.*

Think of your own life and the lives of those around you. I'm sure you can come up with many examples of resolutions that have happened because someone stuck to their guns and was correct in doing so. A friend of mine got a deserved raise because she was ready to quit if her boss didn't come through. Previously, she had asked for raises and never received them because *she didn't mean it when she said she'd quit if she didn't get one.* Or, three patients of mine made successful ultimatums to alcoholic, abusive parents. They wrote loving notes to their alcoholic parents telling them that, although they cared for their parents very much, they could no longer tolerate the pain and abuse they received when visiting and would no longer do so until the parents went into treatment. In all three cases, the patients stuck to their guns and the parents sought help for their addiction.

Knowing how difficult it is to get addicted people into treatment, I was astonished. But after three instances, I realized that all these events had certain things in common. One was that all the parents waited three months to take their giant step. Also, all stepped up their abuse during those three months. They tried every manipulation and threat in the book. One of my patients turned off first her phone and then her answering machine when her father left abusive messages. He then tried to break down her door but left when he heard her call 911. After two months of complete silence came the startling message that he was in a detox center and would stay twenty-eight days for treatment. The other stories were very similar.

## THE THREE-MONTH BREAK

Three months is short enough to still feel the relationship as immediate and vivid, yet long enough to seem like an eternity when you cannot hear or see the loved one's voice or presence. Having no contact for that time period motivates the other person to give up ambivalence and come to a decision about what to do. Of course, the time period could be two, four, or six months, but in my experience, three months most often gives us the answer we need.

Take a common family problem—let's say you want your relationship between yourself and your parents to be more equal, yet they insist on treating you as if you were a child, including using the childhood nickname you've told them you despise. You've tried and tried to resolve this issue but it comes up every time you speak with them. Your Plan A's don't match, and you recognize that you have a Broken Dream.

At this point, I often tell my patients the analogy of the coin. All of us have flipped a penny or a quarter to see whether it comes up heads or tails so we can make a decision, once and for all. Ambivalent relationships have heads and tails also. If you say to your parents, "I feel we have a real difference over how you treat me and we're upset every time we speak to each other. No one is willing to change points of view and it's causing all of us a lot of pain. Let's take a three-month break and see how we all feel after the three months is up." This is a very difficult thing to do, but let's see how a three-month break can tell you the difference between a Broken Dream and a Melt-down.

In deciding to take a break, your parents can feel they don't need to make any changes, but they don't have *you*. And for three months, they'll miss your presence and the sound of your voice. Their fear of changing old habits and always being in the right is now appeased, because you're taking a break. But they don't have a relationship with you either—and we tend to long for what we want and don't have. And having their child, versus having their own way, almost always causes parents' ambivalence to resolve in favor of the relationship.

If you decide not to take a break and go on in the same old way, your parents continue to satisfy their need for dictating the terms between you, but not their need for a child who loves them and wants to be with them. *Then which one do they long for?* Most people and relationships have conflicting needs. And people who have conflicting needs may vacillate forever. You must never be manipulative when you ask for a break or take any other measures in order to help someone decide where they really stand. It should only come after a great deal of soul-searching and a deep feeling of knowing that you really need the thing you're asking for—in this case, the respect of being treated as an adult. Therefore, you must be *willing* to give up your narrower Plan A—a good relationship with your parents (which at the moment you can't get)—for the broader Plan A of a parent-child relationship where *both* sides treat each other respectfully. When you feel centered and firm about this, you may hope and long for your parents to change, but you won't be destroyed if they don't. And while you'll probably feel very sad if they don't, you won't feel crazy or depressed either. If, after the break, they're willing to negotiate shifts in your relationship, you're on your way to fixing your Broken Dream. If they're not, your Plan A was a fantasy and it's time to look at Plan B.

To understand whether your Plan A can be a reality, you must first see whether the other party to the relationship wants it also. If your parents want to share your Plan A of a mutually loving, respectful relationship, it may need to be mended or modified, but keeping the plan can be a realistic goal. If, on the other hand, they choose to continue treating you as a child and refuse to listen to your needs, your Plan A can only be a fantasy. They don't share your plan and don't want what you want. *Plan A is a fantasy when the other party doesn't share your plan's goal.*

Ginny had met the man of her dreams and the relationship was moving toward marriage. She was 27 and eager to get married now, because she wanted lots of children. But Ron was 24, still lived with his family, and was hesitant to give up his freedom and take on these responsibilities. Ginny came from a difficult family situation, and when Ron's loving relatives accepted her with open arms, she realized she would gain not only a husband but a loving family as well.

Ginny decided to tell Ron she needed an answer from him now, or she would have to leave and try to find a man who was ready for marriage. She realized she wanted the Plan A she had always dreamed of, and it was still her most important goal. But Ron was unable to give her a definitive answer.

Ginny decided to wait three months for him to change his mind, as that was the limit of how long she could bear to wait. She came in every week to see me, literally gripping the chair with white knuckles, yet she never called him or got in touch in any other way. During this time, I was mostly giving her support and encouragement and was glad to do so, since I had met Ron and seen the love between them.

Two months and twenty-five days after their last conversation, I got a phone call from Ginny. She had come home from work to find a beautifully wrapped box of her favorite candy on the doorstep. She called Ron and he came over within the hour and proposed marriage. They came in together to see me for premarital counseling and Ron told us what he had felt during that three-month period. At first, he was sure Ginny would call, since she had always been very open and affectionate and he was positive she wanted to be with him. Basically, he said, he was waiting for her to capitulate as she had done before. But as the weeks passed, he began to get more and more anxious, since he missed her and began to realize that this time, things were somehow different. Only one phone call from her, just to say hello, would have erased that "different" feeling because he would have heard the sound of her voice and that would have recalled her presence. *At that point, the "three-month clock" would have begun ticking all over again.* It was the total silence that not only finally convinced him that Ginny really meant what she said, but let him feel how empty life would be without her.

The three-month break helps *both* parties decide whether they want to continue sharing a plan. *You cannot feel good about yourself if you compromise your plan for your life.* You can only feel at peace and happy if you relate to others in such a way as to never compromise the integrity of your Self. Living without fixing a Broken Dream, or living in Meltdown, will cause you to become inauthentic and not the person you sense you should be.

## EVALUATING YOUR DREAMS

To keep your Unsullied Dream or adjust your Modified Dream, you need to do a "quarterly report" to see whether your life is continuing to meet your Plan A or needs to be updated to include natural changes that come with the passage of time. I suggest you keep a special notebook in which, at each change of season, you write down your Plan A's for each aspect of your life. Have pages for Self, Relationships, Family, Work, and Lifestyle, and see how they correspond to the reality you're living. Compare your Plan A's with the months and years that have gone before. Are you on track and heading toward your goals? Or does your quarterly report suggest that you need to modify or change a goal? One person might need to ponder what options are possible when the person she wants to be with is transferred to another state and all the family she loves lives near her.

Someone else might need to realize that there'll be more time now that her children are entering school or going off to college, and how should she spend that extra time? A third might need to keep his eyes open for a new job opportunity, since the company he's loved has been downsizing and he may very well be next.

Modified Dreams can almost always be satisfactorily adjusted if you learn how to go about it. But while they're unresolved, frustration, anger, and misery can enter the picture and lead to further unraveling. Then something easily fixed can dissolve into a Broken Dream or into a nightmare. It's a good idea to ask for advice from trusted friends or relatives, to get different points of view as to how to go about changing your plan. But remember, it's *your* life; after you hear differing opinions, the final decision is yours.

The differentiation that's most difficult to make is to decide whether your dream is Broken and can be restored, or whether it exists only as a fantasy in your own mind. If it can be restored, your Plan A only needs to change direction in order to reach your original goal. *Otherwise, you need to face the fact that you're living Fantasy A, not Plan A, and Plan A is in Meltdown.* Your inside reality isn't matching the outside reality, and you're probably feeling crazy, angry, or depressed.

## WHEN PLAN A FAILS

One sad example in which marriage counseling and psychotherapy did not work, as it most often does, involved a couple who came to see me a few years ago. Justin was a divorce attorney and Coral worked as a hospital volunteer. He was intent on proving how much like his dependent female clients Coral was, and she bought the scenario— Justin as the emotionally healthy, knowledgeable professional, and Coral as the clingy, emotionally unstable, weepy female who was basically sick.

What was really going on was that Justin needed to feel like the "normal" person in a relationship and found a career and a marriage where the other people were "sick." He tended to treat his clients not as ordinary men and women going through an emotionally difficult period, but as basically dependent people who needed to be rescued. Coral was a dependent person, willing to give up her feelings and ideas in order to be taken care of and loved. When they came in for marriage counseling, Justin knew he wasn't the sick one, that it was obviously Coral, and she was the partner at fault in the marriage. Coral *was* emotionally unstable, but the reason was that she believed she was the cause of all the faults and problems in their marriage.

Justin was unable to accept any notion that a relationship is mutual and that both people need to modify their behavior and attitudes to make the partnership work. He only wanted Coral to be "fixed" and then everything would be all right. He dropped out of therapy after eight sessions and told Coral to "get herself well." Coral would come in and report Justin's verbally abusive behavior continued requests for her to leave "his" house. She was unable to modify her Plan A from a need for Justin to love her, in spite of all the facts that showed he didn't, to a need for a spouse to love and be loved by. She would not choose to give up her Fantasy A, which was really about getting her parents' love, and move on to a healthy relationship in the future. Her Plan A could never be a reality—it was only a fantasy.

People aren't masochists when they believe this way. They don't want to live in pain. What they want is to *master* the circumstances, and the formula goes something like this: If I can make Justin love me in my present life, then it will undo the put-downs and lack of respect I felt from my parents and I'll feel like a whole person again. The present loved one (Justin, in Coral's case) then becomes a symbol for our parents—and because all of us need so much to feel loved by our mothers and fathers, we never want to give up trying to get that love. The reason this never works is that if we're acting out of neurotic feelings, we pick someone *identical to our parents—someone who will never be able to give us love.* Of course, all of this isn't in our conscious thinking; it's motivated by past needs we're rarely aware of. It's in these circumstances that people find themselves trapped over and over again in unhappy love affairs and marriages, and it's in these circumstances that psychotherapy so often helps.

Coral understood in her heart that her background gave her fertile soil to play out this neurotic role. Her parents favored her older brothers, and Coral was always made to feel as if they were right and she were wrong. So her relationship with Justin felt normal to her. She refused to attend Codependents Anonymous, which would have given her insight and support, and insisted on concentrating week after week on how she could make herself acceptable to Justin. She was very aware that she had spent her whole life trying to make herself acceptable to her parents, which couldn't be done, yet now she was intent on repeating that role in her marriage. She thought, "If only I try hard enough . . ." The reason this didn't work is that she used radar to pick someone who, because of his own needs, was totally incapable of giving her what she wanted most.

In therapy, people often get to the point where they need to confront their problem where it originally existed—in this case (and in most cases) with the family of origin. If parents and siblings are still alive, then by speaking or writing to them and telling them their present feelings about the past, people like Coral can gradually undo the original knot in the rope, and then the rest of the knot begins to unravel. If parents have died, then this must be done within oneself and it usually is very successful. Though Coral did contact her parents and became less afraid, she refused to have a serious talk with them and played the same childhood role of pretending everything was all right and keeping her real feelings inside. But without untying the original knot, she was unable to see the real Justin she was living with. Instead she saw a Halloween mask of her parents' faces every time she spoke to him and not the real Justin who lived beneath the disguise.

Coral lived not with Plan A, as she thought she was doing, but with Fantasy A, which resided in her dreams but was lived out as a continuing nightmare. Coral eventually dropped out of therapy, and the last I knew she was still trying to get Justin's love, which was still being withheld.

Why would Justin stay in this situation? His neurotic scenario was as follows: Because of his own childhood up-bringing, the only way he could feel healthy or right was to have the other person in any relationship be sick or wrong. As in most neurotic relationships, Coral and Justin's needs meshed and satisfied *both* of them, and so they stayed in Meltdown condition, rather than repairing their marriage—if it could be repaired—and living out a real Plan A in their lives.

## GIVING PLAN A A CHANCE

How can you give Plan A every last chance to be reestablished before you unwillingly conclude it only exists as a fantasy? First, realize that even as you must decide what you want in life, *other people have the exact same right*. Many years ago, I remember taking a course for psychotherapists on how to teach communication skills. It was a wonderful course, taught by Dr. Penelope Russianoff, who certainly had no problem communicating whatsoever. She was a delightful woman and a wonderful teacher. There was much role playing during the sessions, and I'll always remember one young woman who sought help because she thought she wasn't correctly communicating her wish for marriage to her boyfriend. When she was through role playing, we all felt something was wrong, but we didn't know exactly what it was. But Dr. Russianoff did. She said, "*You* have *received his communication, but you don't want to hear it.*"

This is a very profound statement, and one that most of

us don't want to hear. Not hearing what someone said may be why you may go round and round in the same old manner, never resolving your problem because you may not grant the other person—spouse, boss, or friend—the same right you have: *the right to possess his or her own Plan A.* How can you tell whether the other people in your life, with differing plans or differing dreams, will be willing to change or compromise those plans in order to keep you in their lives? How can you tell whether you have a Broken Dream or Meltdown?

It's wonderful to keep your narrow and specific Plan A as long as it works—this particular partner, this particular job, this particular lifestyle and belief system. It's also normal and natural to adjust and fix the parts that need to be changed because of the passage of time, outside circumstances, or the natural ebb and flow of the rhythms of life. Take stock of your moods and feelings; there's a *reason* you're angry, a *reason* you're distressed. Pay attention to those feelings and search for the underlying causes before your plan, which may only need modifying, ends up broken or in shambles. And always be aware that the *broader* you make your Plan A (for instance, "a job that I love and can thrive in," rather than, "*this* job, which I must succeed in no matter what"), the more satisfied and successful you will be. Finding a broader Plan A may fix a Modified or Broken Dream, but if the broader plan also doesn't work, *your plan is in Meltdown, and unless you want to lead a life of dissatisfaction and misery, you need to find Plan B.* Doing so will enable you to live a life that will lead to satisfaction and your Authentic Self. In other words, it will enable you to live a meaningful life that respects and fulfills your deepest and healthiest needs.

Hard as it is to realize your Plan A is a fantasy and you need Plan B, it's impossible to do so if you're still stuck and wishing, "If only . . ." Before you're able to find Plan B, you need to Get Unstuck.

# GETTING UNSTUCK:
## The Need for Plan B

No life is fulfilling unless it is meaningful. But the meaning of your life may be quite different from your neighbor's or mine. However, if you're like most people, you're probably too busy to take the necessary time to stop and reflect on what your unique purpose is meant to be.

Together, we make up a community. And just as communities need the specialized services of people who provide us with food, clothing, and shelter and the distinct aid that teachers, police, and physicians provide, so too must *you* find the unique role you're meant to contribute to the world around you. A few years ago, I read a question that startled me. The question was, *"What is the purpose and meaning of your life?"*

It's a very profound question to ponder. And if your conclusion is that the path you're on—your Plan A—isn't satisfying your purpose and never can, you need Plan B. Your life is *meant* to have purpose and meaning, and the goal of your journey is to search for, discover, and live out that goal. For Plan A to be satisfying, it must encompass your purpose; if it doesn't, then *Plan B is the solution to restore the meaningful life that Plan A will never provide.*

When you have a Broken Dream or your dream has reached Meltdown status, it's time to consider Plan B. Chapter Three will show how choosing Plan B may not only transform your life but your spirit as well. And when a real trauma occurs, the knowledge that you *need* Plan B may be your only pathway to breakthrough, recovery, and peace.

## Is Plan B Right for You?

Most likely you know about the concept of Plan B and even use the term in daily conversation. But it's probably a new idea to think of it as leading to permanent solutions for the problems you face. Take the following quiz and see where you stand in terms of awareness of your need to seek a new path to a meaningful life:

1. Are you involved in inauthentic roles? Are you false in relationship to yourself, your partner, your family or your job, or are people false to you?

2. Are you guilty of ignoring signals that something is wrong or "off" in the situations you're involved in?

3. Do you disregard facts that need facing, and push them aside instead?

4. Are you unwilling to look at new ideas and believe that "this is the way things are"?

5. Are you unhappy in your life and do you feel you were born that way?

6. Do you believe you'll never achieve the goals you long for?

7. Do you feel you don't *deserve* to be happy?

8. Do you suspect there's something in your background that prevents you from being your genuine self?

9. Do you go around in circles and never find the way out?

10. If your life ended now, would you regret what you've left undone?

The more times you responded yes to these questions, the more likely it is you're living an inauthentic life—a life untrue to your genuine self and your real goals and aims. Even one yes means there's an impediment to becoming your Authentic Self; the more there are, the more emphasis on your need to get unstuck and move on in a new direction.

This quiz is helpful for other reasons. We really *do* want happiness—and not in the ways most of us spend time looking for it. Shopping is not the purpose of life; neither is promiscuity, perfect independence, living beyond one's means, or any other forms of overindulgence. Anyone who has spent months or years pursuing these goals knows how empty and barren they become. Although questions 5 and 7 speak of happiness, Plan B is not about seeking the superficial happiness of temporary pleasures. *It's about finding the deep-down satisfaction that comes from discovering and living out the purpose and meaning of your life here on earth.*

Another important use of the quiz is to see how much past trauma is keeping you stuck in an unhappy life. Any one of your yes answers may be due to conscious or unconscious reasons that prevent you from moving forward, but pay special attention to your responses to questions 7 and 8. If you answered yes to either of these questions, set aside time to think through the probable causes of your response and try to make connections between your present unhappiness and your past experiences. If, after a period of time and talking it over with a trusted teacher, friend, or pastor, you find these connections don't help you untangle present problems or alleviate your pain, consider psychotherapy. It may help you get over your "stuckness" and start you on your life's true path. Therapy is helpful when past occurrences damage your self-esteem so much that you feel "bad" and feel you don't *deserve* Plan B. If that's so for you, professional counseling will help you get unstuck and explore the reasons for those false beliefs. Then it should be possible to find the beautiful person who exists underneath all the rage, anger, and despair—the good person you really are who deserves life's gifts.

Being happy is intimately linked to becoming the particular person you're meant to be. I often use the "botany analogy" to show people I work with how unique and special they really are, and how important it is to use that uniqueness to find purpose and meaning. Let's suppose you were meant to be a rose but you're trying to live the life of a tulip. Since you can't succeed, *you are stuck and you're going to fail.* The only possible way you can get unstuck and be successful is if you live the life of the rose. This may seem to be a simple analogy, but the reason one flower can't bloom differently than it does is that genetically it doesn't possess the ability to do so. It is impossible to be something you're not, but many people are excellent at pretending they can, and continue to attempt living a life that's a lie.

I often say to my accountant as I watch him fill out form after form, "If there's a hell, that's where they'd put me—behind that desk." He usually responds, "And if there's a hell, they'd give me your job!" Neither one of us has been unfortunate enough to choose the wrong job. When you choose an inappropriate purpose for your life or an inappropriate meaning, you're living a false life—a life untrue to yourself. Then you'll find yourself without the ability or resources to get unstuck and find correct solutions, and you'll fail. Trying to be someone other than what you *can* be is to live with the Plan A of being an inauthentic person. It's living with the knowledge that something's dishonest in your life. Deciding to become the person you were *meant* to be is to get unstuck, move on, and find your Authentic Self. And that's what Plan B is designed to do.

Let's assume you've looked carefully at your Plan A and have discarded it as being unworkable for the person you are and the life you're meant to lead. You've realized you'll be permanently unfulfilled if you don't change the basic assumptions you've been operating with. You've decided to put Plan A behind you and search for Plan B, because you know you finally need to get unstuck. Plan B allows the seed carrying the blueprint that is *you* to blossom.

But seeds need the correct amount of fertilizer to grow; your seed may have been buried by too much manure, enough to prevent light, rain, and air from ever reaching you. As you grew up, poor choices or terrible traumas may have choked off the graceful, emerging bud. By starting over and taking charge of your garden with the correct ingredients, attention, and care, you can find the Plan B that allows you to be *you*. Just as it takes time for a tree to grow or a flower to bloom, so will it take time for you to figure out and evolve into the individual you were intended to be. That growing and evolving should always lead toward fulfilling the purpose and meaning of your life.

In order to find that meaning, begin paying attention to your thoughts, feelings, and physical reactions as you go through your daily routine. *Pay attention to being unhappy.* If you're not at peace, you have a problem; if you're depressed, you have a problem; if you're anxious, you have a problem, and if you're not enthusiastic about life, you either have a problem or are heading for one in the future. Addictions, headaches, digestive problems, or other bodily symptoms without physical cause are signals for you to look at the ingredients your present life is composed of, and find the ones that are emotionally painful for you.

Pay attention to your gut feelings. *Gut feelings are hardly ever wrong.* Pick up on the signals that particular people and events inspire in you. I tell everyone I work with—young and old; single, gay, or married—to *see* everything and *hear* everything that happens to them. If a red flag goes up, if someone says or does something that seems slightly off, *pay attention to that fact.* You won't be wrong. *Character* may be an old-fashioned word, and everyone does something out of character once in a while. But if red flags go up two or three times, the person, family, or situation you're involved with has a character *different* from what they're trying to project or different from what you want to believe.

What have gut feelings to do with Plan B? To find solutions for your life and become your Authentic Self, you must communicate from the bedrock of your own beliefs, values, and truth to the bedrock of another's. There can be no room in your life ever again for game playing or manipulation. Negative gut feelings occur because you have subliminal senses that pick up cues that you may be in jeopardy—that the other person may be manipulating the truth between you. Animals use these cues to protect their children's lives and their own. Deer and birds flee, not when they're *sure* the hunter is near but when they *sense* he is. This gift has been given to you, too—but do you always use it?

Many people distrust their most genuine feelings because of low self-esteem. They think so little of themselves and their abilities that when a genuine feeling comes their way, they automatically think it must be wrong and discard it. Yet over and over again, as I work with people struggling toward a healthy life, I see that their gut feelings are over-whelmingly correct. One of the reasons people with low self-esteem are so often stuck is that they ignore the signals they receive to run and leave bad situations. They remain entrapped because they agree they must be wrong when another person tells them so. It's like the deer trusting the hunter when the hunter tells him he's just out for a stroll, instead of saving his very life by bounding away as fast as he can to get out of harm's way.

When you've paid close attention to your gut feelings and acknowledged that certain relationships repeatedly up-set you, you may recognize you've felt stuck for a long time. But that very knowledge may *keep* you feeling stuck, since the essence of "stuckness" is not to know how to get out of your quandary and move on to a better life. Understand-ing that there can *be* a Plan B proves you're not quite as stuck as before. The very fact that you know a Plan B is possible—even though you don't yet know what it is or how to find it—means you've come a long way from being stuck. *Really being stuck is living with a Plan A that's wrong for you and thinking it's the only choice you have.*

Recognizing the need for Plan B may be the single most important step you take in changing the life you're living, yet *don't* want, to the one you're not living and *do* want. Sara found this out as she struggled with repeated rejection and failure in her work, family, and romantic life.

*  *  *

I first met Sara on Wall Street, where we both were speak-
ers at a seminar entitled "Stress Reduction in the Work
Environment." During a break, Sara confided to me that
she felt like a fraud since she was probably experiencing
more stress in her work and home life than most people
who were sitting in the audience. She made an appointment
to see me, and at our first meeting told a long story of woe.
Though Sara had a high position in her company—director
of communications for a training corporation—she feared
she was about to lose her job because of office politics. This
was the third company she'd worked for where she was at
the losing end of political maneuvering, and Sara felt there
must be a pattern in this due to something within herself
and not to random political jockeying.

Her romantic relationships followed the same pattern.
After six months to a year, men left her and she never
understood why. At 37, she'd been divorced twice and desperately wanted to find a man with whom she could spend
the rest of her life. With her parents, brother, and two
sisters, misunderstandings and arguments abounded. Sara
usually found herself in a minority of one, with the others
arrayed against her.

As Sara explored her background, she began to make
connections between her behavior in her work and personal
life and her family history. Her parents had divorced when
Sara was three, and her mother remarried a man who never
learned to like his stepdaughter, let alone love her. Sara's
mother and stepfather had three more children, and Sara

was handed the role of outsider and family scapegoat. Though she was the oldest, baby-sat the younger kids, and performed many household chores while the other children did none, she was always considered "wrong." This had two lasting effects. The first was that she believed it, the second was that even though she felt inadequate, she was a fighter who strove to prove she was "OK" and "right."

Sara worked extra hard at school and at work to be accepted; in the beginning, her perseverance always paid off. Her performance was superior and got her noticed and rewarded. She was valedictorian at her college graduation, and a communications company hired her and put her on the fast track. Then, for the first of many times, things began to fall apart. In the safe atmosphere of the therapy sessions, Sara began to look objectively at what had happened. She recognized she'd been defensive whenever her boss had suggestions or criticism, and she always needed to win arguments with colleagues. Within her first year, many people felt uncomfortable around her or openly disliked her. She was able to resign and found increasingly powerful jobs in other companies because her work was outstanding and her bosses gave her excellent referrals based on her production. But too many moves in too few years was telling, and if Sara lost her present position, there'd be no way to continue her upwardly mobile course.

At this point in therapy, Sara understood *what* was happening at work, but she still didn't understand *why*. It's understanding the "why" of things with our hearts and not just our heads that leads to untangling the chains that hold us fast to old, outworn patterns. *It's emotional understanding and not intellectual understanding* that leads to the "aha!" that changes our lives. So Sara struggled on and began to observe her romantic patterns as well. She discovered she was attracted to men who seemed aloof and didn't need her. These relationships developed in the first place because Sara worked very hard to get boyfriends intrigued and involved with her. She was usually able to do this in the short run, when the affairs were in their early stages, but was unsuccessful in the long run, as the men she chose always needed their emotional distance. After a while, the closeness Sara wanted and needed repelled them and they ran away from her. So she experienced rejection over and over again, just as she did while growing up.

Finally, Sara took a long hard look at her family life and how she was still treated as the outsider and scapegoat in all their interactions. She wanted desperately to be accepted by them and especially by her mother, yet try as she might, this never occurred. Sara knew intellectually that she could never change the family pattern, but like so many people, knowing didn't stop her from attempting again and again to do so. As she continued her work in therapy, she finally understood *emotionally* that her Plan A would never be fulfilled, and a Plan B was essential. She understood in her heart that in trying to get unavailable men to love her, she was repeating the original pattern of trying to get her mother and stepfather to notice and love her. It didn't, because she had to pick the same type of person in order to undo the wrong—a person who wouldn't or couldn't show her love. When Sara met loving men who were interested in her, she found them "boring" or "not macho enough." They didn't fit her script and so she was doomed to disappointment *until she changed that script.*

When Sara understood this she became upset and felt that, since she knew she *needed* to change, she should immediately know *how* to do so. It took time for her to understand that change is a process; it takes a while for new ways of thinking and feeling to settle in and become comfortable. And what needed to settle in just then was the deep conviction that change was *necessary*. Once this process had taken place—and it took a few months—it didn't take long for Sara to change her life.

I've found this pattern true over and over again. The long hard work is coming to grips with the *need* to change. Once that hard work is done, the course of therapy or marriage counseling usually is rapid. And that's what happened to Sara. Finally, she could consciously write a script—her Plan B—that would enable her to love and be loved, and be successful as well. The new script she chose was one where she was a person who deserved love and success in spite of never having received it. Once she truly felt she deserved success, her work, family, and romantic situations resolved to reflect her new self.

## Understanding Why a New Plan Is Necessary

When you feel your old plan won't work anymore, your first step should not be to cast about for a new one. Your first step should be embracing the idea that *a new plan is necessary*. It's mind-boggling to entertain the very concept of change; time—days, weeks, or even months—is required to assimilate that huge idea and let it settle to a deep conviction within. Don't allow yourself to worry or compulsively ask yourself what to do in order to *implement* the change. That comes after you feel, without a shadow of a doubt, that change is *required*.

Feelings operate within an emotionally logical system, just as thinking operates within an intellectually logical one. Emotions respond to fear of danger even more than thoughts do. And what causes more fear than abandoning a pattern that's worked for you—no matter how badly—and switching to a new one that has unknown results? Remember, your fears are there to help you survive, and the new pattern is untested. So emotional logic tells you you've survived very well thank you, just the way you are, and you'd better not change a thing. You tell yourself the tried and true has worked—and the proof is, you're still alive. So you need time—as long as it takes—to work this through within yourself. You need time to *emotionally* understand that the real you—your Authentic Self—will never exist unless and until you make a decision to change. *And that decision will enable you, for the first time, to be who you really are.*

The converse of this is that when you grasp the truth that you need a Plan B, you're also facing the fact you're living a life that's not working for you. And it may not have worked for a very long time—even forever. This issue of identity—of who you've been so far and who you want to be in the future—is the very foundation of change, and deserves all the time it takes to allow yourself to go step-by-step through this important process. Much of this process takes place in your subconscious, which asks, "Can I do it?" "I can't do it!" "What if I did do it?" and keeps you sifting through endless fears, possibilities, and challenges. One day, without realizing how you ever got there, you'll wake up with the answer: not only the absolute certainty that you *can* change, but the knowledge that you *must*.

## THE NEED FOR CHANGE

Claire and Austin were teachers who met the first day they were assigned to the same suburban middle school. They soon married, bought a handyman's special, and spent the next several years remodeling. Five years later, they celebrated the completion of their home by taking a long summer vacation and after returning, bought a dog, acquired a cat, and settled down to start a family.

Two years later, no children had come. By this time, they were in their mid-30s and beginning to feel the pressure of Claire's biological clock. After many tests, Claire had a minor operation that they hoped would enhance her fertility, but six months later nothing had happened. After six more months of fertility drugs and multiple office procedures, the only choices left to them didn't have a high rate of success and were extremely expensive. They were ambivalent, upset, and exhausted, and at this point they decided to come for marriage counseling.

Claire took a seat at one end of the sofa, and Austin at the other. Their body language and tight lips told me more than words how isolated they felt from each other. Austin began speaking and told of the closeness and intimacy they used to enjoy—sharing the same interests, laughing and loving while building a life together. Claire agreed, saying that the only ingredient missing from their dream was a house full of children but the lack of that dream was poisoning their marriage. She felt desperate and was angry at Austin for refusing to try the next step on the infertility ladder—a $12,000 in-vitro series that had only a modest success rate. He argued they'd used up much of their savings to restore the house and didn't want to further deplete their bank account. Claire felt they should beg, borrow, or steal—do anything that might provide them with their wished-for children.

Trauma and loss cause so much stress that marriages often begin to fail under their weight, and this was certainly true of Claire and Austin's. Sex had long ago ceased being fun and had instead become a duty. Life had lost its savor, and conceiving a child was an obsessive desire that drove away other happiness. As long as there remained a next step, the hope, the wish, and the dream continued. But as each step failed and the next became more tenuous and expensive, the more pressure Claire and Austin felt and the more anger and blame they displaced onto each other. They had spoken of options such as foster parenting, adoption, or remaining childless, but both were adamant that none of these were acceptable, and only their own biological child could bring them happiness.

Americans live with the expectation of happiness. We've had half a century of rising expectations and a very bountiful national existence. This, combined with our belief that as individuals we can accomplish anything we set out to do, and that hard work will always be suitably rewarded, leads us to expect success as our right. Even our Constitution states we're entitled to the pursuit of happiness. Since Claire and Austin were playing by the rules, they believed that everything in life *ought* to work out for them. They believed it was unfair to find problems or tragedy they couldn't overcome. And since they couldn't figure out who to blame—because who *is* to blame for life's tragedies?— they began to blame each other and things went rapidly downhill.

As long as Claire and Austin railed against their fate and insisted on childbearing as a right, rather than the biological lottery most people can expect to win, they were stuck in a thought process that could never succeed. They felt all the classic symptoms people feel when mired in stuckness and failure—irritability, frustration, guilt, blame, obsessive thoughts, anger, and loss of pleasure in each other and the world.

After two months of marriage counseling, they decided to give up their fertility quest. They felt that the emotional roller coaster of alternating hope and despair was destroying them and their marriage, and they'd rather live a childless life than face divorce. Austin and Claire still wanted their own biological child and refused to consider alternatives, but agreed it was better to live an empty life than their current one of tension and estrangement.

They were surprised to see that this decision left them relieved. They'd anticipated a great deal of depression, but,

unexpectedly, it never appeared. Instead, as Claire described it, they both felt as if they were recuperating from
a long illness—lethargic, empty, depleted, but feeling better than when in the grips of the ailment. As we discussed
this emptiness, Austin compared it to "crying uncle" in a
schoolyard fight. In the second grade, a bully had beaten
him, and when he couldn't stand the pain anymore, Austin
gave up. Though he felt defeated before himself and his
classmates, the reality of the bully's size and strength was
clear and he knew he'd have gone home more bloody and
bruised the longer he continued. So, he had felt relieved
and had no desire to continue the fight.

The analogy was a good one, because once they faced
the reality of their infertility, they stopped getting emotionally beaten. At this moment, infertility for Austin and
Claire *was* the reality, since they decided they'd depleted as
much of their financial assets and more of their emotional
ones than they could really afford. They sadly agreed that
even if they'd been wealthy, they had no more emotional
capital to spend.

The previous few months of a last frantic attempt at con-
ception and the more recent ones of emptiness and deple-
tion were periods of mourning, which most of us go
through when we're losing people or dreams we love. Anger, scrambling to save or cure, intense pain, accepting the
reality of the loss, and secret feelings of relief that the
struggle is finally over are universal ways of grieving. But
after grieving, when we're ready to greet life anew, we're
no longer stuck. Mourning cleanses us and allows a new
dream—Plan B—to enter the place where our old dream

dwelt. Once we discard the fantasy we can't have, it leaves an empty space where a new, possible Plan B can be born and grow to fruition. *As long as old dreams live in our hearts, there's no room to entertain new hopes, new thoughts, or a new future.*

Claire and Austin continued counseling for four months after they made their decision to discontinue fertility procedures. During this period of "recuperation," they felt that their dream had died and one of the chief purposes of their marriage had disappeared. The focus of the sessions shifted from dealing with the fears, conflicts, and emotions of battling infertility to reconciling with each other and the loss of their dream. One day, Claire made a connection between her refusal to consider other methods of enlarging their family and the fact that her father, John, had also clung to only one method of living out his dream.

Twenty years ago, when Claire was a teenager, her father had lost a thriving grocery store when he refused a supermarket's offer to buy out his business and busy location. Though they offered John enough to retire, or to open a gourmet shop down the street, he loved his business and wanted to live out his dream unchanged. Her father refused to update his life's plan with changing times, and ended up in bankruptcy as the supermarket opened nearby and usurped his business.

Claire's father now works as a store manager, resenting each and every day that he's an employee and not an owner. Her mother deals with his anger and bitterness by emotionally withdrawing and staying away from home as much as her volunteer activities allow. All Claire has heard since the grocery store and their financial security disappeared was how she should stick to her dreams and make them work. Claire had learned the lesson well, but it was the wrong lesson.

Claire's father wouldn't or couldn't update his Plan A of owning a prospering grocery store. Since he didn't want to retire, he could have accepted the supermarket's buyout and invested the proceeds in a little gourmet shop. There was an unfilled need for one in the town and, with his experience, it probably would have been successful. Instead he lost everything—money, status, purpose, self-respect, and a happy family life—all because he hung on to his dream *in its original form*.

After Austin and Claire explored the impact her family experience had had on Claire's approach to life, and acknowledged their own expectations that hopes, wishes, desires, and dreams would be filled as ordered, they were ready to explore their present options and priorities. They found that their mutual anger had diminished and been replaced by sorrow. They began to feel closer as once again they gave each other comfort. Their marriage improved, but they missed the excitement and enthusiasm of a joint goal. Little by little, they faced the fact that the home they'd lavished so much love and attention on would remain childless unless they considered alternatives previously rejected. Over a period of time, Austin and Claire realized they *did* want the house filled with children they'd always dreamed of. They rejected the idea of being foster parents, since as teachers they see the boys and girls they grow fond of move on every year. They're now exploring avenues of adoption and want two children of their very own—a phrase they had previously used to mean genetic offspring only.

Claire and Austin discarded their Plan A of having their own biological children and chose the Plan B of adoption they had previously rejected. In order to reach their new plan, they had to go through the process of trying everything within their means to accomplish their original Plan A. When they finally agreed their plan was in Meltdown, they needed time to mourn the loss of their dream. Finally, they were able to explore new options and find Plan B.

Claire and Austin now stand a good chance of fulfilling their dream—a slightly different dream, but one that embodies the concept of "having, at last, a home filled with laughing, loving children," as Austin put it at our first meeting. If they'd continued to insist on biological children and been unable to get unstuck from that desire, they would have ended up with a shattered dream, just as Claire's father had. Getting unstuck from Plan A freed them to explore new options and arrive at Plan B. Now, instead of a childless home, they've salvaged their dream and are working toward filling their house with the laughs, shouts, and cries they've always wanted to hear.

If you realize that you too need a Plan B, how will you find it among infinite possibilities? How can you distinguish a plan that leads you to your Authentic Self from the myriad of others vying for your attention? The plan you want is the one that takes you directly to your solution.

# IMPLEMENTING SOLUTIONS:
## Choosing Your Plan

Now that you've made a definite decision to find Plan B, how can you assess the myriad possibilities that occur to you? It's delightful to think we have infinite choices, but in reality it's confusing and frustrating to confront more than two or three options at a time.

A good way to begin searching is to use the question, *"What's the Solution?"* This simple sentence could save more friendships, marriages, jobs, and family relationships than practically any other.

The Solution-Oriented Life consists precisely of asking this simple question and doing some thoughtful intellectual *and* emotional reasoning that helps you find the correct answers for your self. When you're stuck in Plan A, you either don't think in terms of solutions, or you think there's only *one* "solution"—the non-solution that hasn't worked. Now that you're ready for Plan B, it's important not to go from considering only one solution to considering an infinite number. Considering too many options is guaranteed to overwhelm you so much that you'll be stuck in Plan A forever. Yet if you don't consider a wide variety of plans, how can you assess all your options? If there's a Plan B, what about Plans C, D, F, and Z?

## FINDING A SOLUTION

Before we go on, take the following quiz and see how good you currently are at implementing solutions to your problems:

1. Do you have issues that need addressing, but you've not thought in terms of solutions for them?

2. Do you have "tunnel vision" in choosing solutions and select the first plan that occurs to you?

3. Do you tend to choose the easiest plan and not necessarily the one that's best?

4. Do you solve problems the same way your parents did, when you know they weren't good at finding solutions to theirs?

5. When trying to solve problems, can you think of only one solution and it's one you don't really want?

6. Do you find yourself going round and round with two or three "solutions" that just don't work?

7. Do you tend to find too many options, and that confuses you?

8. Do you and a spouse, friend, or family member each stay stuck in your own position and not think of other solutions satisfactory to *both* of you?

9. Do you and someone close to you understand that if you can't agree on a joint plan, you need a third way or there'll be continued friction and anger between you?

10. Do you realize that choosing a different plan right now might solve a current problem?

Answering no to questions 1 through 8, and yes to questions 9 and 10 is an excellent indication that no matter how many problems come your way, you've got superior skills in finding solutions to them. If one or two of your answers were yes to questions 1 through 8 and no to questions 9 and 10, reading the different solution-seeking methods in this chapter may be all you need to set you on the right path to solve your present dilemmas. But if three or more of your answers were yes to questions 1 through 8 and no to questions 9 and 10, the techniques that follow may not be all that's necessary to find and implement good solutions for your life. If that's so, future chapters will give you further clues as to how to formulate plans that will help solve your present problems.

To help pick the winner of your Plan B sweepstakes and implement that winning plan, Chapter Four explores six different methods to help winnow your search to a reasonable few. And it's from these two or three most promising options that you'll choose your plan. The six methods are (1) Research, (2) Prioritizing, (3) Brainstorming, (4) Productive Daydreaming, (5) Journal Keeping, and (6) the Third Way.

## 1. RESEARCH

Research is a very straightforward method that helps you eliminate a plethora of choices and focus on a very few. It consists of techniques you naturally think of when hearing the word—using the library or the Internet, for example. But many people neglect to think of research in a very simple, yet powerful way: interviewing experts and valued family and friends. Helpful experts may be either professionals in the problem-solving field or people you know who've been through similar situations—they're experts through experience.

For instance, if you've recently moved to a new city, and need to find a local doctor, you could call the nearby hospital and get a referral. Or you could ask your neighbors who they use, and whether they're satisfied with their choice. The more neighbors who enthusiastically endorse the same doctor, the more confident you'll be in choosing that doctor as your own. You've certainly done something like this many times in your life, but you may not have realized this same process is valid in implementing solutions for difficult problems as well. Asking divorced friends for names of attorneys, discussing their experiences with dating again, and asking how they handled their children's anxieties is research every bit as valid as using the reference library. In fact, it's often more helpful since you can clarify things you don't understand by extended discussion over a period of time.

It's usually a good idea to conduct research on all fronts—the more formal type, using books, computers, and professional expertise, as well as consultation with family, friends, and colleagues. For instance, Conrad and Anne were a couple in their 50s who had just found out their son, Hank, was gay. He was now in his 30s and felt he could no longer live a lie. He'd finally come out to his parents when he came home for his annual vacation. Conrad and Anne held very conservative social and political views. They told him, truthfully, that nothing could change the love they had for him, but they were upset and confused by the lifestyle they felt Hank had deliberately chosen.

Hank had done some research on his own and so was able to steer his parents to books and support groups that might be helpful to them. When his parents began their own investigations, they got some conflicting messages. Their minister told them that Hank was sinning greatly, and some books he suggested they read about homosexuality reinforced that message. They were so disturbed by this that they went to the library and read every book they could that dealt with the current knowledge of the effects of genetics and environment on determining homosexuality. Most of their research told them that the choice of whether or not to be gay is not one that people freely make, but rather one they find thrust upon them.

The more they read, the more they came to the conclusion that Hank did not *choose* to "sin," but was gay and had not chosen that lifestyle deliberately. Their research led them to believe that homosexuality was not solely determined by the genes, and understood that childhood and adolescent experiences could also contribute to one's being gay. But they completely rejected the idea that Hank had chosen to be homosexual in order to rebel against his parents, his community, or his religion.

By researching all manner of books and magazines and conducting searches on the Internet, Anne and Conrad were able to reject the viewpoint that their son was sinning and could change. Instead, what they accepted as truth was that Hank could not and would not change, and that they would have to struggle with the turmoil this created within themselves. For that, they needed to conduct research on a different front.

Again, Hank was able to steer them in the right direction and led them to a support group consisting of family members of gays and lesbians. There, Anne and Conrad were able to share with others who had experienced the same feelings: grief over the knowledge that they'd never have grandchildren, and guilt and shame for feeling they had done something to create his "gayness." This support group, composed of other parents and relatives who had lived through these same experiences, were able to substitute hope, comfort, and solid facts for the fears and guilt Anne and Conrad were suffering.

Researching a situation helps you assess your options realistically. But remember that the person you're doing the research for is *you*. Your parent or best friend, studying the same information, might choose a different alternative that would be correct for *them*. Each person is unique, so your choice may be very different from theirs, but the situation might be a disaster if you chose another's plan. It's very important to listen to your own needs and implement the choice you've arrived at after a thorough investigation. Conrad and Anne could have chosen to agree with their minister that their son was deliberately choosing to defy God. Instead, their research led them to an acceptance of Hank's gayness and relief that they could still believe he was a good and decent person.

Many men and women never explore all their options or even think in terms of solutions, such as fixing Plan A or choosing Plan B. *Fear* is the most common reason why people don't explore their options, but exploring them usually decreases the fear. For example, they may be in a miserable marriage and want a divorce, yet hesitate to get one for economic reasons. But they never consult an attorney to see the probable financial outcome. Never having done any research, they live with a global fear. If they do consult with a lawyer, the fear they'll live with need no longer be global, but the more defined one of actual options. *Living with realistic fear is a necessary step to digesting it, overcoming it, and moving on toward Plan B.*

Knowledge helps eliminate fear. I asked one woman who dearly wanted to separate from a wealthy husband who constantly abused her, why she stayed. She said she was afraid of the financial consequences of divorce. He'd told her she'd get nothing. I suggested she have a consultation with a good attorney who could tell her what her actual status would probably be. She refused and in exploring her reasons for refusal, discovered a very common mistake. She believed that consultation would force her to take the next step and file for divorce when, psychologically, she wasn't prepared to do so.

She was also afraid of going against her more knowledgeable husband and believed him when he said she'd get nothing. I suggested that research could help her find an excellent divorce attorney—and he or she would not be afraid to take on her husband. Finding an excellent attorney, doctor, accountant, or therapist can be one of the most important areas of research you'll ever undertake. It's easy to see the difference between a mediocre doctor and an excellent one. In divorce cases, finding an excellent divorce attorney can be the most important research you tackle.

*Remember, taking one step at a time and never taking the next step until you're ready and willing to do so can eliminate fear and the paralysis resulting from it.* It can enable you to finally get rid of the Meltdown in your life and find a Plan B that lets you live in peace.

## 2. Prioritizing

Prioritizing is a useful method to find a solution when there are only a few plans to choose from. Let's suppose you live in San Francisco, have a thousand dollars saved for a vacation, and would like to visit either Australia or the Pacific Northwest. Your budget will quickly help you choose the Northwest as your first priority—Australia will have to wait. If the priority is your budget, the choice is easy. But let's suppose your priority is to see strange wildlife. Then kiwis, koalas, and kangaroos make the Australian trip win hands down, though you might have to wait until you've saved more. Without a priority, you could go round and round—"It's cheaper to visit the Northwest but the koalas are so cute," and so on and on. By prioritizing budgets and wildlife and choosing one or the other, your choice becomes easy and eliminates days or weeks of treadmill thinking. When it's difficult to choose one plan among one or two attractive alternatives, ask yourself, *"What's my priority?"*

Let's take another example. Lydia had been seeing me for relationship problems and was nearing the end of therapy. She'd lived and worked in Manhattan for ten years and was ready for a more peaceful life. She found New York too hectic and her solution was to move to a quieter locale. She was able to state her problem and her solution for it quite easily, but had difficulty choosing the particular plan that would activate that choice. Her Plan B was realistic since she worked as a manager in a large HMO and her skills were greatly in demand. She'd received job offers from companies located in Florida, Georgia, and Massachusetts, but found it difficult to come to a decision.

The offers were similar in salary and working conditions, so Lydia decided to base her choice on location. She liked Florida for its warm weather and beaches, Georgia for the

HMO's Atlanta location, and Massachusetts for its nearness to her old hometown. She was doing what so many people do, going round and round with treadmill thinking and not getting anywhere. When I suggested she write down beaches, Atlanta, and being with old friends and family and list them in order of importance, two weeks' worth of obsessing instantly dropped away. She quickly and easily placed close relationships first and realized that beaches and Atlanta were a very distant second and third. Before prioritizing, Lydia thought she'd pick a job based on pleasant geography and warm weather; after prioritizing, she realized family and friends were a far more important factor. When she prioritized, choosing to live near her old hometown clearly became Plan B.

When you have two or three possible choices from which to choose Plan B, those choices may seem confusing unless you list your priorities and then rank them in order of importance. Most times one preference will stand head and shoulders above the others, since your priorities won't have equal weight. In the minority of cases, where, after ranking, you realize you must satisfy two or three priorities, you may be able to combine your choices in a satisfactory way. Lydia moved thirty miles from her family and friends and rented an apartment in Cambridge. She was in a much smaller, quieter city than New York and felt she'd meet single people her own age, yet was still near to the suburban town full of people she felt close to. Lydia was able to satisfy three priorities—being near family and friends, living in a quieter city, and finding a new job she liked.

### 3. BRAINSTORMING

Brainstorming is another method to help you choose Plan B out of the many options that might help you solve your problem. The essence of brainstorming is to write down *as many* solutions to your dilemma as you can possibly think of, without judging which are best until all are included. Silly solutions as well as outlandish ones, far-fetched ideas as well as thoughtful ones, are all put down on paper. Only after the last possible solution is written are the ideas reassessed in light of their chances of success in the real world.

Joanne, 35, and Keith, 39, were a childless couple who were having financial difficulties. Although they were both well-established in sales careers, and had a combined yearly income of $130,000, they spent a great deal and had no plans for their financial future. At this point, Joanne wanted to move from their townhouse to a large, single-family home being built nearby, and Keith had been longing for a thirty-four-foot sailboat.

When I first saw them, they'd been arguing over whether to put a hefty down payment on the house or the boat, since they realized they didn't have enough money for both. Their arguments had grown worse over the past few months and were beginning to become bitter. They said they needed me as a referee to help them make a decision. Each was entrenched in wanting their own desire; they "knew" only *that* desire could make them happy, yet recognized it was wrong to let materialistic things interfere with their love.

I explained to them that I wasn't a referee or judge; my

role was to help them learn how to make their own decisions without anger or arguments. They understood that all decisions had to be mutual and wholehearted or there'd be recriminations—and they didn't want their marriage undergoing more stress and strain.

I explained the concept of brainstorming, and they agreed it might help them choose in what had become an impossible decision. They each consented to do the following: (1) Make separate lists of all the things they wanted in the next twenty years, without showing each other their lists; (2) rearrange their individual lists in priority order; (3) exchange lists to see if any of their top five priorities matched the other's; (4) estimate the annual cost of the top five items appearing in both lists; (5) add up the costs, and (6) think about what they discovered without discussing it until our next session.

The next week, they had bemused expressions on their faces as they discussed how many "wants" had appeared on their lists; how important each "want" was; and, more than anything else, how expensive all these desires were. Children were first on their mutual list, though they didn't wish to start a family for another year or two. Travel was also a high priority, as was living in an upscale suburb. A gracious home was on both their lists, but the sailboat was on Keith's list only.

The original reason they'd come for counseling was to help them decide which Plan A to choose—the house or the boat. Brainstorming helped them focus on their basic values and by doing so they saw they'd have to make choices between material acquisitions and starting a family.

Their bemused expressions had resulted from adding up the enormous outlay their priorities would cost each year—far more than they could realistically afford, even by earning higher commissions and making increased sales. They'd been living their lives as so many affluent 30ish couples do—satisfying more and more needs and desires without adding up the accumulating financial, emotional, and spiritual costs.

By using the brainstorming method, they were able to get down to the nitty-gritty of their lives—how to choose a plan that would satisfy not the superficial possessions they thought they wanted, but the deep desires of their hearts. By going through this process, they discovered they'd been living their lives on a materialistic, fairly superficial level. Basically, they weren't shallow people and were slightly ashamed of this discovery. Over the next few weeks, it led to many fruitful discussions between them about their basic value system.

Brainstorming had allowed them to include *all* their desires, and in doing so had shown them they were following a path that would lead them away from their deepest desires and dreams. While they could afford two or three items on their agenda—a lovely house, the fine suburb, frequent travel, or two or three children—they'd be bankrupt trying to have them all. Brainstorming helped them focus on their basic values, since they saw that their current choices favored consumerism over family and children.

What gets so many couples like Keith and Joanne into trouble is the conscious or unconscious mindset that they *deserve* to have everything. Again, we see that most Americans who were born after World War II (everyone who is 50ish and under today) have grown up feeling that life *ought* to include all the goodies, since that's the way life's been for the last fifty years—most Americans' entire lifetime. And it's easy now to actually *have* our material desires satisfied with credit cards and easy financing.

Luckily, Keith and Joanne were able to take a sober look at their lives before they found themselves head over heels in debt and becoming the type of people they didn't want to be. Their original problem had been choosing between a house or a boat, and that predicament happily led to reviewing their life's goals together. Brainstorming made them aware that neither the house nor the boat would lead to future gratification, since their top five priorities were (1) children brought up (2) in an excellent suburb (3) in a larger home than the one Joanne was now contemplating (4) with tuition available for excellent universities and (5) money for travel throughout this entire period.

When I pointed out they'd be over 50 when their children graduated from college, and retirement plans weren't even among their top priorities, both Keith and Joanne became upset. It took many weeks of hard work for them to come to terms with the fact that they couldn't have it all—that life only offered them choices, which could end up being much more painful ones than these. They went over and over their prioritized list and were willing to give up nothing. Yet they grasped the fact that retirement was an issue at least as important as travel and large homes.

Finally, after living with the pain of losing their dream and mourning the loss of that dream—their Plan A—they were able to come up with a realistic plan. Since the result of their new brainstorming was placing a high priority on a secure retirement—something that hadn't even *appeared* on their list of "wants," their other goals had to shift. They realized their original brainstorming hadn't been complete, since it hadn't carried them far enough into the future. Their impulsive desires and need for instant gratification had led them to obscure what would happen to them in that future—old age and their need to prepare for it. All of us have to balance our needs for instant and delayed gratification and all of us do it differently. But the necessity for balance is always there, and brainstorming all the facts of life will help you, just as it helped Joanne and Keith, find a satisfying Plan B to help you move toward your life's true goals.

What they realized after the gloom of mourning their lost big dream was that though they needed to *shift* their goals, they didn't need to abandon them. Wanting their original goals in their original form would have led to eventual disaster. But because they were thoughtful people at heart, they understood that their materialism was leading them down a path they really didn't want to follow.

I spent the next month helping them compromise between their desires and their pocketbook. They both planned to put much more into their 401K plans, which would help them build up tax-free retirement income on a forced savings basis. They found themselves actually chuckling after a visit to their accountant, who told them they'd be retirement millionaires if they were just a little more careful now. Joanne explained they each were allowed to put up to $13,000 a year into their retirement plans, and that total of $26,000 would be matched by 50 percent more donated by their companies. That came to $39,000 per year, which invested at 8 percent would yield over $1.6 million if they retired at age 62, and over $2 million if they waited until age 65. With such big numbers in their future, they decided to do the exact opposite of what they had first planned to do—they decided to reduce their cost of living by the sum needed for their 401K accounts, instead of increasing it that amount by buying a larger house or a new sailboat.

One way Keith and Joanne reduced their costs was their decision to eat out only once a week instead of the three or four times they'd drifted into. They were shocked that their restaurant bills had been so huge and figured they would save approximately $5,000 yearly. They saved another $5,000 by taking a camping trip instead of the European vacation they'd originally planned. Reducing purchases of clothes, theater tickets, and computer gadgets added up to another $5,000, and trading in their BMW and Infinity (they really *were* living a trendy lifestyle) and buying a two-year-old Honda and a year-old Camry would do the rest.

They chose to stay in their townhouse and invest the down payment they would have spent, as well as the higher housing costs of a more expensive home. That would enable them to buy a good house in a good suburb five years from now. That image of the good house in a good suburb replaced the old idea of the grand house in a grand suburb that had been their Plan A. They still hoped for children and wanted to start their family a year or two from now, and were planning one long camping vacation to Europe during the next summer. Though they still hoped for top colleges for their undoubtedly brilliant future offspring, Keith suggested investing in their state's college tuition plan. This allows parents to prepay college tuition at a reasonable rate and then lets their children attend any state schools they qualify for. Initially, Joanne didn't like this idea, but finally agreed to it since it was a fall-back position, was affordable, and gave them peace of mind because the money was refundable if Keith, Jr., or Joannie were admitted to Harvard after all.

They also recognized that though they couldn't afford the *QE II*, they could plan delightful and much less expensive vacations every year or so if they cared to. In short, they learned a very significant lesson—*they could have a deeply meaningful life encompassing all their most important goals and desires if they gave up unrealistic thinking and fantasies.* Brainstorming enabled them to choose a detailed Plan B that they tailored to fit their dreams. All their desires were included in a new plan that was no longer based on materialism. It was a plan no longer so grandiose as to be unrealizable, unaffordable, and likely to cause big financial and emotional problems in their future.

Brainstorming has a particular usefulness in helping people find a Plan B that gets them to their genuine goals. In Keith and Joanne's case, they thought their goal was to help them choose between two material desires. But brainstorming is at its most useful when you place the desire you *think* you want among all your other needs and desires and then rank them in priority order. As this couple learned, it may help you face your real values and you may end up with entirely different priorities than where you began. It's an eye-opening way to find out what you really want in life versus what you think you want, and helps you move from more superficial values to more fundamental ones. Joanne and Keith's plan did just that. They had been living a Plan A they had never thought through or deliberately chosen. Brainstorming helped them consciously select a Plan B that encompassed all they truly wanted and also fit the larger needs of a more mature and thoughtful couple. Their arguments ceased and they looked forward to implementing the goals they had jointly chosen.

## 4. PRODUCTIVE DAYDREAMING

Productive daydreaming is another method that helps you choose Plan B. *It's a method of alternating between fantasy and reality that leads to achieving goals and reaching dreams with the greatest chance of success and the smallest possibility of failure.* Obviously, it's not good to spend hours daydreaming if it interferes with daily tasks. It's important to make the distinction between fantasy that's used to *conceptualize* future changes—a sort of "what if" daydreaming—and fantasy that's used to *avoid* real life. If you want to start your own business, it's obviously smarter to use fantasy to conceptualize about different methods of doing so than to go through two or three aborted attempts in order to find a real-life formula that works.

This brings up a point that often gets people into trouble—continuing to daydream without discovering what their options are. It's understandable and essential to begin daydreaming by fantasizing about owning your own business. But when you've fantasized long enough to know that is your Plan B, *you must do research to back up your plan.* The next step in productive daydreaming is finding out all you can about the business you'd like to start—how necessary is it in your area; what's the competition; how to do marketing and distribution; how many employees are needed, where to locate, and usually, most important of all, how much capital is required to get it off the ground. Fact finding, interviews with others in the field, and networking are all fundamental at this stage and are the very opposite of daydreaming.

Once you have as much information as possible, it's time for daydreaming again. Remember, getting unstuck involves *living with the concept of change*; your research will have flooded you with the knowledge that change after change is necessary. So it's time to shift gears again and go back to freely fantasizing about every available option. Some will seem inviting; others may frighten you. Live with them all for awhile. After a time, the inviting ones may seem less so and the frightening ones may not be as fearful. In fact, often the most frightening scripts turn out to be the ones we really want.

Once you've researched your options and daydreamed about them long enough, you'll find one of them beginning to emerge as the winner of your Plan B sweepstakes. Now it's time to do research again, using the same factors mentioned earlier—demographics, marketing, and so on. Afterward, when you've got your ideas plotted out precisely, it's time to daydream once again and then live with that concept for a time.

People make mistakes, depending not upon whether they daydream, but rather whether they do so exclusively. And it's just as easy to make a mistake by not daydreaming at all. Remember, our gut feelings and our unconscious come into play when we fantasize—that's where either the "aha!" response or the terror comes from. All the meticulous research in the world won't help if you've got the right idea but are terrified of implementing it. Either you'll make mistakes because your emotions don't match your thinking, or you'll be slowed down by your fears and unable to proceed with the strength and energy you'll need to succeed.

In order to implement a solution—in this case, having your own business—you must choose a plan, and in order to choose the *correct* Plan B, you need to entertain all your options. Productive daydreaming helps you do just that. By alternating fantasy and reality—your daydreams and your research—you are allowing all aspects of yourself to be involved. You're not just a logical thinking machine and you're not just an emotional bundle of protoplasm either. No matter how successful you've been at burying one aspect of yourself, you're both a thinking and feeling human being. And the way you'll grow into your Authentic Self is by integrating the two halves of your emotions and intellect. Productive daydreaming does just that in a way that helps you combine and balance these two important elements—the elements that make you *You*.

## 5. Journal Keeping

Keeping a journal is another effective method to help you choose one solution from the many available to you. This boyfriend or that, this career change or that one, whether to give up an annoying friendship, and how to handle difficult relatives may all be solved through writing faithfully in a diary or journal. And the more open and honest you are about your feelings—the more you use your journal as a trusted friend—the easier it becomes to see where your heart is leading you.

Keeping a journal has three primary purposes: to become an ongoing record of your daily doings and your emotional life; to have a cathartic effect by enabling you to vent feelings of joy, anger, sorrow, hope, love, and frustration; and to help you see what path you're on as you periodically review what's written. All these purposes can be helpful in implementing solutions for your problems and dilemmas.

But beware—keeping a journal can also be a trap. In adolescence, many young people pour out emotions in a dramatic way that seems to enable them to cope with the profound changes involved in becoming adult. Yet when I see adults keeping journals for years and years, they don't always provide that same service. There's a difference between keeping a diary or journal during a crisis or stressful times and using it to wallow in negative emotion for years.

Journal keeping is useful if it's utilized to see where you've come from and where you're headed. Putting pen to paper helps to make sense of chaotic events and overwhelming emotions. But beware of misusing long-term writing in order to flounder in negative feelings and to maintain a status quo that doesn't work. Beware of feeding off hurts and pain instead of becoming aware of a need to lessen or eliminate them by finding solutions to the reasons they exist in the first place. Beware of writing for egocentric reasons and only considering the "I" and not the "you" of relationships and the larger world surrounding you.

As you review your journal over a period of weeks and months, become aware of what your problems and feelings are. Do you view your job as repetitious or stressful? Are your friendships fraught with spitefulness and negativity or with happiness and replenishment? Do you see life as boring and meaningless or exciting and fulfilling? Finding a pattern in what you write can help you reflect on the direction your life is taking. Are you moving toward your goals? Do you even know what your goals are? Discern the pattern of your life by reviewing your journal to see how you deal with the difficulties you face. Do you get mired in them or do you flounder awhile, then pick yourself up, dust yourself off, and seek solutions? Use your journal to help you find what you seek.

## 6. THE THIRD WAY

Most people know from personal experience or at least have heard of the methods of problem solving already discussed. But very few people know or practice a method that is often the *only* way to find satisfactory solutions. I coined the phrase *the Third Way* because naming something makes it a recognizable tool to use in finding a Plan B when you disagree with your boss, colleagues, family, or friends.

Gina and Jeremy have been in marriage counseling for three months because of constant petty arguments. They want to trade in an old car and buy a pickup truck they've longed for. Jeremy wants a red one and Gina wants the dark green model. Each feels pretty strongly about wanting his or her own choice and equally strongly about not wanting the other's. Most couples in this situation end up with either the red or the dark green pickup, which means that one person is happy and the other isn't. The problem for *both* people is that the winner is pleased with the choice but never pleased with the resentment and anger radiating from the loser. *And that's what happens when one person wins and the other one loses.*

In many marriages and partnerships, there's often a dominant partner who makes decisions for the couple. But if the other partner doesn't wholeheartedly agree, and just acquiesces to avoid an argument, low-level resentment and anger build. Multiply this by the many large and small decisions of daily life and it's easy to see why so many couples are constantly arguing and sniping at each other—bickering over where to place the coffeepot or when to take the dog out. They're not even aware of what the underlying cause of their bickering is—they've been dealing with the sneeze and not the cold. *The hidden cause for so many petty arguments between family members is an underlying factor they're not aware of and not the thing they think they're fighting about*. And that underlying factor is very often a scenario where one partner habitually wins and the other one loses.

Since Gina and Jeremy's marriage was structured so that Jeremy did most of the decision making and Gina just went along, agreeing only to keep the peace, she ended up losing over and over again. Her resentment built layer upon layer until she periodically exploded and a volcano of anger erupted. Between the bouts of violent anger, low-level resentment was always present. (Do you recognize your own marriage here? You might, since this is a very common scenario.) They were both unaware of the underlying cause of her explosions and their arguments and so hadn't a clue as to how to change the unhappy interaction. Jeremy would state that Gina was a "crazy lady" and dismiss her—another common male reaction—which would only enrage Gina more.

Through marriage counseling, they were able to discover the hidden cause of their arguments and learned that the Third Way would give them both what they genuinely wanted. Gina learned to use the Third Way and say to Jeremy, "I don't want the red truck and you don't want the dark green one. So if we can't agree, we need to choose another color we'll both find acceptable."

Most people don't think of this solution. They remain entrenched in either/or thinking—*either* the red *or* the dark green truck—and leave all other options unexplored. Either/or thinking is win-lose thinking; either Gina wins and Jeremy isn't happy, or Jeremy wins and Gina's stuck driving a truck whose color she doesn't like. But Gina and Jeremy did learn the Third Way and ended up with a silver pickup they both enjoy. Because they learned to use this method to solve most other disagreements, they also each ended up with a loving partner who wasn't constantly picking at the other over every minor issue.

Jeremy's color choice for the pickup was his Plan A. Gina's choice of color was *her* Plan A. Their Third Way was a joint Plan B. What this really boils down to is this: Gina and Jeremy's bickering was the result of their Plan A in its Broken Dream form. (Jeremy would lead and Gina would follow and they would both be happy with that way of life.) When they weren't happy, they were unable to alter their interaction and Plan A broke down. But when they opted for the Third Way, they chose a Plan B of married life that became harmonious and fun-loving again.

Another example of the Third Way: Jeremy wants to go to a war movie. Gina wants to see the latest romantic tear-jerker. Neither wants to compromise and so they stay home, angry at each other and feeling cheated. That's their old Plan A mode. Plan B's Third Way might be for Jeremy to go to the romantic movie this week and Gina to go to the war movie next week; for each to go to the movie he or she wants alone; for each to go to the desired movie with a friend instead of each other; and so on and so on. There are so many solutions when we use the Third Way and focus on both partners winning instead of only one of the partners. And, as you can see, brainstorming is an excellent method of finding a Third Way that's the most acceptable scenario for both.

Though the Third Way is especially useful in finding successful solutions between two or more people, it's also effective in helping a single individual choose the best plan. Cheryl, a 25-year-old market researcher, was dating two men, Joey and Paul. Joey was in the recording business and offered her an exciting lifestyle, while Paul was an assistant bank manager who lived a much more sober and stable life. Both were kind and loving and both wanted to marry her. And she cared a great deal about each of them. She came to see me for consultation when she couldn't make up her mind about which man to marry.

After a few weeks, Cheryl discovered that she usually looked for polar opposites when dating—she'd never encountered a man who embodied excitement *and* stability and didn't even know that it could exist within one person. Since she wanted both in a partner, when she found someone who possessed one of these qualities, after a time she felt cheated of the other. Part of our work together consisted in helping Gina see that she felt lacking in both these characteristics and saw herself as both unstable and dull—a combination that clearly lowered her self-esteem.

When we explored where these ideas came from, Gina spoke sadly of her brilliant but erratic father who was unable to hold a job. Her mother tried desperately to keep the family together by mending clothes and serving leftovers day after day; to Gina, her mother was dullness personified. She *knew* she wasn't as drab as her mother, but she also lacked inner feelings of stability, since she'd never known them in her own home. It became obvious to her that she depended on others for those qualities she felt missing in herself. She worked hard on this issue and came to a point where she felt entitled to generate healthy ex-

citement, such as a fun-filled birthday party for her sister
and a vacation on a freighter heading for Panama for herself. She also recognized that she needed to develop a sense
of stability within herself and, in the course of treatment,
moved from an apartment she shared with two roommates
to an efficiency apartment where she could better control
what went on in her own home.

As her therapy progressed and Cheryl felt stronger and
more centered emotionally, she became disenchanted with
*both* men as marriage partners. Though she felt genuinely
fond of them both, much of the attractiveness each possessed were qualities she no longer needed supplied from
the outside. Then their other attributes came to the fore—
qualities that often go along with excitement or a too-sober
way of looking at the universe. She began to be more an-
noyed at Joey's abrupt changes of plans and his habit of
not following through on his promises to her. At the same
time, she became even more bored at the plodding way
Paul lived his life. After a few more months, she realized
she could never live a lifetime with either of them and
parted from both. Cheryl ended up with a deep conviction
that if it meant waiting forever, she could only marry a man
who was both exciting and stable. She was ready for the
Plan B of a Third Way—not the either/or choice of a man
who was dull and sober, or one who was exciting and irresponsible, but a third type of man—a mature person who
would embody all the desirable qualities Gina felt were important in a lifelong partner.

Many men and women feel that to choose a stable partner, they need to choose Boring. That is definitely not true.

Or they feel that to have an interesting partner in their lives, they need to settle for Irresponsible. That's not true either. Mature people can encompass all aspects of personality; once Cheryl became more mature herself, she realized she couldn't and needn't settle for less in a spouse.

So many of us find ourselves stuck in life, going round and round in treadmill thinking trying to find a plan that will work, when the *method* we're using precludes any plan from being successful. It's only when we learn a totally new method that a solution becomes at all possible.

If you're using treadmill thinking to find solutions without success, perhaps your Plan A is at fault. See whether by using one of these methods you can find your Plan B and the Solution-Oriented Life. Whichever technique you finally choose—and more than one can be utilized in order to choose your plan—all six methods really boil down to a few principles: (1) Do enough research to open up your world to all viable options. (2) From this myriad of options, choose a few worth considering seriously. (3) Explore your interests, beliefs, and values in depth so that you end up fulfilling your deepest needs rather than gratifying more superficial ones.

To learn this new habit, practice implementing solutions for relatively easy problems in your present life. These principles work for *every* area of living and once you understand them, you're ready to move on and discover how to find solutions for more difficult problem areas, including those of self, relationships, family, work, depression, anxiety, and the truly desperate circumstances of living. Once you learn how to implement solutions to these troubling problems, you'll be able to live your life full of the purpose and joy that's your right to deserve.

# SOLUTIONS FOR SELF:
## Reclaiming the Real You

Our mind, heart, body, and soul make up the components of what we view as our Self. In the past decade or so, people have become much more aware of the need for exercise and nutrition in increasing the health of our physical bodies. As a consequence, not only our life span but our vitality throughout that span have increased to the longest in human history. But have we used the same dedication in taking care of those other elements of our Selves—our minds, hearts, and souls? Surely not.

For these non-material aspects of the Self to be as healthy as your physical body, your thoughts and feelings must be healthy also. The same attention that's focused on physical exercise must also be focused on your inner Self.

People are accused nowadays of being self-centered and egotistical. But in paying attention to yourself, we're not speaking of self-centered behavior. Rather we're speaking of paying attention to who you really are and your purpose in being here on earth. And that kind of attention leads *away* from selfishness and points toward your becoming your Authentic Self that others are drawn to because they see that you possess a secret they hunger for.

Most people don't even think of spending time looking at their motives, feelings, and actions. In fact, with all the differing roles we play, there's less and less time for introspection, and when something has to give, it's often care of our Self that goes first.

Chapter Five will teach you how to reclaim your Self— the Authentic Self that never plays games or manipulates because it would violate that very Self to do so. When you care for your Self and live a life true to your talents, gifts, and real desires, it becomes possible, perhaps for the first time, to reflect on the thoughts and feelings coming from your very center. Some call that center the Unconscious, some the Spirit, and some the Soul. But whatever you choose to call it, unless you're true to that innermost part of your being, your beliefs, actions, and relationships are shallower and more distorted than you'd like them to be. However, when you *do* act from that centered place, your moods, emotions, words, and deeds all become one—they flow from the real you. Then there's a wholeness and oneness to your life instead of fragmented and conflicting thoughts and emotions.

The previous chapters have helped you recognize the problems you have and helped you think in terms of solutions for them. And these solutions need to come from that innermost center so they reflect the authentic person you really are and not an inauthentic one you may think you need to be. Now that you're ready to implement specific solutions, those solutions *must* come from your Authentic Self. What kind of answers would you have for your life if they came from your inauthentic Self? You can see from the very phrase how awful that would be. Yet that's where many people's solutions do come from.

## ARE YOU YOUR AUTHENTIC SELF?

This quiz will help you see if you habitually act from the centered or a non-centered part of yourself:

_____ 1. Do you hold your thoughts and beliefs with quiet conviction, or do you feel unsettled or confused?

_____ 2. Do you convey quiet conviction to others when you express those ideas?

_____ 3. Do you know where you're going in your relationships and are you happy or at peace with where they're leading?

_____ 4. Do you know where you're heading psychologically, emotionally, and spiritually and are you glad about the path you're on?

_____ 5. Do you feel centered and content no matter how difficult your present circumstances?

_____ 6. Do you feel depressed and unhappy even though your life is going fairly well?

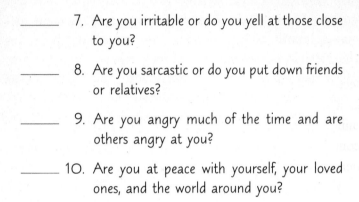

_____ 7.  Are you irritable or do you yell at those close to you?

_____ 8.  Are you sarcastic or do you put down friends or relatives?

_____ 9.  Are you angry much of the time and are others angry at you?

_____ 10. Are you at peace with yourself, your loved ones, and the world around you?

If you answered yes to questions 1 through 5 and question 10 and no to questions 6 through 9, you're leading a life true to the person you want to be. Whether or not others agree with you, they know where you stand. Again, even if you answered no to questions 1 through 5 and question 10 or yes to questions 6 through 9 only once, look into that matter, because it points toward an area in your life that you don't feel settled about. And if you answered two or more questions in a non-centered way, your life is probably not going the way you wish it to be.

Notice a very important point. Someone may answer all of these questions in the centered mode, and be an opinionated, domineering, and completely disagreeable person. They may be so self-righteous that they allow no other thought, opinion, or need to even occur to them. We're not talking of this kind of person, though—instead, we're speaking of your Authentic Self who would always entertain new ideas and knowledge and be open to the thoughts, opinions, and needs of others. These thoughts may ultimately be rejected if they're not pertinent to the path you're on, but it's very necessary to consider others and to periodically reexamine your basic beliefs and values. Doing so helps you see whether you're continuing to grow intellectually, emotionally, and spiritually. The Authentic Self is always growing, and growth takes place when more building blocks are added to the existing structure; these come from continued additions and reflections to your innermost life.

The time you spend examining the thoughts of your heart, mind, and soul will ultimately be exhilarating. You'll become acquainted with a beautiful person—you—who may have been hidden for a very long time under layers of heaped-up garbage. The Authentic Self, who's coming from the most central part of your being, is a person who has no need to ever lie, manipulate, scream, or be sarcastic. This self can calmly and quietly state the truth both inwardly and to any other person. No one ever has to yell the truth and no one ever has to maneuver around it.

This sounds like Nirvana—and in a way, it is. Once you achieve inner peace, your whole world falls into place. You know what your agenda ought to be, and you go about putting it into practice. Boredom and purposelessness fall away and energy and happiness are restored. But don't worry about things getting too Nirvana-like. We all live with enough pressures and frustrating circumstances to ever enter the realm of bliss, at least in this life—though it's possible to live in that blessed state for short, ecstatic bursts of time. The story of Louise will help you see the transforming effects of becoming your Authentic Self.

## REVISING YOUR LIFE

When I first met her, Louise was a divorced 64-year-old woman, living in a large, suburban home. She was a retired music teacher and lived with her two unemployed sons, ages 29 and 32. She came to see me because of a depression that she couldn't seem to overcome. Louise became one of the most inspiring women I've ever had the privilege of working with. Yet in the beginning, she was living a life that was as false to her true Self as it was possible to be.

Because of her depression, I suggested she see a psychiatrist and inquire about antidepressant medication, but Louise refused. She wanted to work on her issues without medication, and at the time her depression didn't seem that severe. Louise told me she'd worked as a music teacher in the public schools for thirty years and had hated every minute of it. She'd been married five times, had had many lovers, and was now involved with one who was helping her financially. She didn't love this man and was with him for economic reasons only, and when I gently suggested that's what prostitutes do, she didn't want to hear it. Louise hated where she lived and wanted to sell her house and move into a condo—a smaller place where her two sons couldn't follow. They prevailed upon her, however, to stay where she was and continue to support them on her pension, which wasn't very much at all. They told her they were looking for jobs, but neither one worked and hadn't in the last three years.

Louise hated everything about her life and had for a long time. Her Plan A was to suppress her needs and wishes and subordinate them to those of others so they would love her. But all they did was use her and disrespect her. Her Plan A was in Meltdown, as was Louise. By living a life she hated, she was living a false life—an inauthentic life. So it was natural to feel depressed and, feeling that way, she isolated herself from everyone but the few people she was involved with on a day-to-day basis. And, unknown to me, she drank to numb the pain.

People who are alcoholics are invariably liars and manipulators. They may lie by omission only, but that's still a big lie. A few months into treatment, I sensed that something was wrong, but Louise denied it. I gave her my home telephone number anyway, not something I usually do, and told her to call me anytime if she really needed to. A week later, my phone rang at 10:30 on a Saturday night, in the middle of a dinner party. And it was lucky that I was home.

Louise was at the other end of the line, crying and almost incoherent. She had been drinking heavily and was standing at the kitchen sink with a handful of barbiturates she had secretly collected and was ready to swallow. The only Plan B she could think of was to kill herself. I told her to hold on and used three-way calling to dial the local police, who came and took her to the hospital. Louise was hospitalized in the psychiatric unit for ten days and began to attend AA meetings while she was hospitalized. Those ten days changed her life.

I visited, and told her that the only way we could continue to work together was if she agreed to be under a psychiatrist's care for medical purposes and also agreed to attend at least three AA meetings a week for a month and then two a week for as long as she was in therapy. Louise did agree; when she came to see me again, she expressed relief that all her secrets were now on the table. This was a very important moment, because both in and out of therapy, two adults need a relationship that is honest and works for *both* of them.

Louise was correct in thinking that if she told me about her active alcoholism, I wouldn't see her in treatment. That's because my training and expertise are not in addictions counseling, although I do see many recovering alcoholics. But they have stopped drinking and either are in or have been through recovery programs. Louise knew this and was keeping something hidden that would change our relationship if I found out about it. That's exactly the kind of association she'd always had with people. No one clearly stated their true position and then negotiated with the other person so that a *mutual* decision could be reached. Instead, all her relationships were devious and manipulative.

This was our first topic of discussion, and Louise began to see that relationships could be honest, different, and *better* than she'd experienced. If she'd told me about her addiction, I would have said she could continue to drink as much as she wanted—she was free to do so—but what *I* needed from our relationship was a person who committed herself to recovery and worked on her problems. *No one can be practicing addictive behavior and get anything at all from psychotherapy or counseling unless that addictive behavior is also addressed and dealt with.* Otherwise, she was wasting my time and her money. I stated that I had the right to decide to work with her, just as she had the right to decide to work with me. All relationships must be mutual and reciprocal; if they're not, there's something wrong at their very core. Many people learn about honest relationships for the very first time with a trustworthy psychotherapist or counselor.

Louise came in at the next session and declared, "I'm at a revision point in my life," and indeed she was. She made her decision to recover and began attending AA meetings, and then began to make real progress in her life. Note that I didn't force this decision upon her. She was a free person who made a free choice and, happily for her own sake, she chose healing. Now that our relationship was mutually truthful, Louise could compare it to other relationships in her life and find them wanting. She was tired of pretending it was okay for her sons to be unemployed, when she was using her sparse resources to support them. She discovered she was tired of going to bed with her lover but rationalized that he sincerely wanted to help her financially, and going to bed with him wasn't part of any unspoken deal. I suggested she entertain him as always but leave out the sex, and see what happened. Of course, he left no money.

Without the alcohol to cloud her thinking and let Louise drown out her problems, she had to face the facts. And the facts were that she was living a life false to her inner Self, and therefore she was false to everyone around her.

At 64, Louise didn't have a clue as to what being true to herself meant. She wanted and needed a healthy Plan B, but didn't know what that plan should be. As is the case with so many alcoholics, Louise was brought up in an alcoholic home. Her mother drank heavily and her father told her never to let anyone know what went on at home. There are always family secrets with addictive families, and so Louise grew up lying to friends and pretending to them and to herself that everything was all right. Once she was set on that path, she never learned to tell herself the truth and became unable to distinguish her true needs as she began to make her life's decisions.

One thing she needed, as all of us do, was her mother's love. Since her mother was usually drunk and oblivious to her surroundings, Louise was neglected and longed to be cherished. Because of this, she made poor choices with every one of her husbands, who all fell into the same category. They loved her because she was pretty, docile, and eager to please, and she was this way in order to win their love. They were interested in having a wife who would go along with whatever they wanted, but were not particularly interested in pleasing her. When she did voice her own wishes, she was shot down in often sarcastic or brutal ways. Things always went downhill, with both parties becoming dissatisfied, and none of her marriages lasted longer than seven years.

Louise made a vow to herself that she would never again do anything that didn't feel deep-down right to herself— and she kept that promise. This vow became the cornerstone of her Plan B. That meant she didn't do anything at all for awhile because she didn't know what in the world she really wanted. When I reminded her that she'd like to sell her house and move into a condo, she recoiled with fear. Playing the role of peacemaker in her alcoholic family while growing up had conditioned her to that same role as

an adult. So when her sons tried to control her by becoming angry when she suggested they move out, she backed
down and kept the peace by allowing them to remain. But
she paid the price of depression and addiction for this behavior and all the other situations she gave in to without
really wanting to do so.

The relationship that Louise and I developed was the
first mutually respectful one she'd ever had in her long life.
For the first time, she was able to learn a healthy pattern
in interactions with others. I was honest with her and told
her when I disagreed with something she was doing, but
though I rejected the behavior, I never rejected *her*. She
came to trust me and knew I was in her corner. She saw
for the first time that a healthy relationship doesn't end
when one person disagrees with the other, and neither one
need give in at the expense of their own beliefs and values.

After months of struggling, Louise came to accept that
if I could value her as a person worthy of respect, she could
learn to respect herself also. That fact too became incorporated into Plan B. The first thing she did was tell her
lover he was welcome to visit but there'd be no sex anymore. He began to come over less often, and then, when
he saw she wouldn't change her mind, stopped visiting entirely. At first, Louise felt hurt and betrayed, but learned
from this experience to pay attention to her gut feelings
and interactions with others. What she learned was that she
had used her lover to get money and he had used her for
sex, and that she'd been as guilty as he was. All of Louise's
relationships had been manipulative ones where she used

and was used by others. She finally recognized she was tired of this scenario and that it served no healthy purpose.

Without her lover's cash, Louise was short of money. We went over her budget together, and she decided to cut down on her considerable spending at the mall. She'd done this to be "nice" to herself since she didn't feel anyone else was. Once she cut down on these unnecessary expenditures, she found she'd almost made up for the loss of her lover's cash. This experience gave her the feeling of control over her own life for the very first time. It was a heady experience, and Louise began to have a sparkle in her eye and a lift to her step for the first time since I'd known her.

Making only one change in your life can help you see that you really have the ability to control your world, and once you experience that feeling of control, you'll be able to make another change and still another, until, lo and behold, you've made so many changes that your life itself has changed for the better. And you're giving up an outworn Plan A as you do so.

So it was with Louise. She felt so much better after she rid herself of one manipulative relationship that two months later she put her house on the market and informed her sons they had three months to find other living arrangements. None of their old tricks worked anymore, because Louise *meant* what she said, which she'd never done before. She had finally given up her Plan A to give in to others in order to try to receive their love. She recognized this as a failed strategy that had led to a life in Meltdown and near suicide.

Both of her sons tried to use anger, guilt, and the silent

treatment to get Louise to cancel her moving plans, but to no avail, as she saw their behavior in a clear light for the first time. She felt angry at herself—and sad, too, that she'd given in to them over the years. She saw her own part in their behavior by keeping them as companions because she had so few others in her life. She understood that her own needs had contributed to their inability to function as adults, and they needed to start holding jobs and having their own families. In short, she saw she'd actually be doing them a great favor by kicking them out of her house, no matter how angry they became.

Louise did move into her dream condo—one with a small place for flowers instead of the large yard she previously had to care for. That was another thing she'd done—despite repeated requests, she'd ended up taking care of a large garden without any help from her sons. After a few months of planting flowers and making the condo cozy, she began to feel bored. Since her sons and lover were gone, Louise found she had no one in her daily life. She began to reach out to one or two of her fellow AA members and went out with them for coffee after the meetings. Over a period of time, she began to make friends who, for the first time, had no interest in her company other than for herself. This acceptance was another milestone on the road to Louise's reclamation project—the fact that people could like her and seek her out, not for what she could materially provide them, but for her companionship and company alone.

Now Louise was on a roll, and the next thing she did was join a small orchestra at the local senior citizen center.

She'd played the cello for many years but put it aside as her depression grew. The daily practice sessions and the twice-weekly rehearsals filled her life with the music she loved and led to more friendships. Within six months of joining the orchestra, Louise decided to have a party for all the new friends she'd made both at AA and through her music. She went into a momentary panic when she thought of her guest list of twenty people but eventually decided on a Christmas open house, where eggnog and her special cookies would be the centerpiece.

This was the first entertaining Louise had done for decades and was a tremendous milestone in her recovery process. She fought her old issues of perfectionism and inadequacy—people would see her home and find it wanting, or would compare her entertaining skills with Martha Stewart and find they didn't measure up. And of course, her standard *was* to compare herself to Martha Stewart. Our sessions together were spent exploring the reasons for her fears and perfectionism and giving her the support and encouragement she needed.

At last the time for the party arrived and I couldn't wait for the next session to find out how Louise had managed as a host. I didn't have to wait for her to say anything— her demeanor said it all. She was glowing and spoke again and again of how surprised she was at how much her new friends had enjoyed themselves; they raved about her decorating and cookies and asked her for the recipe. She could see that their compliments were genuine and told me how she had finally relaxed herself—with nonalcoholic eggnog— and had a grand time.

There was one final issue that Louise wanted to resolve before she left therapy, and that was the one involving her spiritual life. I've found that when people discover their true Self, they deepen their spiritual life also. That doesn't necessarily mean following traditional religion—rather, it means including themselves as part of the larger universe and then finding their place in it. For many people, that means deciding to follow established religious beliefs and joining an organized religion. For others it comes to mean faith in God without any dogma or church attendance— and still others just come to hold the conviction that life is precious and the world beautiful and full of wonder.


## SPIRITUALITY AND THE SELF

The importance of spirituality in reclaiming your Authentic Self is that you come to feel you fit into successive communities and all those communities nourish you. Perhaps for the first time, you fit into a community of one—your own company. Most people who've never discovered their own deepest needs and followed their own special talents and gifts have never enjoyed time spent alone with themselves. Indeed, many people hate that company and do anything and everything to avoid it, including busyness, affairs, drugs, alcohol, and workaholism.

Next, you come to fit into a healthy companionship of family and friends. If you've enjoyed this in the past, you continue to do so, and if you haven't, you begin to, either by changing the relationship patterns between you and those close to you, or by finding a new family and friends who are both healthy and functional. Many times, as people regain and reclaim themselves, they find that old friends no longer satisfy their needs and they leave unhealthy relationships behind. This is where joining a community of people who share the same spiritual and ethical values you do becomes so important, because this is where new family and friends can come from. It's also important because that new community gives you the opportunity to live out the beliefs and values that are intrinsic to the real You. It's relatively easy for people who join a religious community to meet new people because they gather together on a weekly basis, and there's often a coffee hour in which to socialize.

If you don't opt for traditional beliefs to live out your spirituality, it's essential to find a group or society that expresses the same interests and values that you have, and get involved in that way. It could be a political or environmental group, a charity that works hard for a cause you believe in, or a cultural group that joins together to produce or appreciate beauty.

Louise's spiritual trajectory went as follows: At first, she chose an agnostic AA group since she wasn't religious. Because AA has a spiritual base, many groups are overtly religious and Louise couldn't relate to them. So she found a group where no one practiced a traditional religion. But as her recovery progressed, she found she was looking for a spirituality that had a more formal structure. She investigated some local churches and found one that suited her needs and eventually switched AA groups to one where spirituality had a place in the meetings. Louise was happy with her choices, made friends, and became involved in her congregational community.

This is an important point. You've learned to choose Plan B when Plan A fails, but if you live your life in a mindful way, Plan B often *evolves* as you continue on life's journey. In Louise's case, she was sure her plan was to be the irreligious person she'd always been, but as she became her Authentic Self, she felt a need to explore and fulfill a spiritual side of herself that she didn't even know existed.

I've also found this to be true for people who never develop a formal religious life. As they allow their deepest needs and feelings to develop, they find wonder and awe inside themselves for the larger beauty of nature and the universe. What's happened is that for the first time, they feel part of a larger plan and feel connected to the Creation outside of themselves. And this is the largest community we can belong to. When you're comfortable and intimate with your own company, then with that of family and friends, then involved in the larger community of town, country, and nations, and finally feel connected to Creation itself, you will be your Authentic Self. And living a life true to your Authentic Self is the ultimate aim of the Solution-Oriented Life.

Finally, Louise formulated her Plan B. Her plan is "to live a life honest and truthful in all relationships and to fulfill my physical, financial, emotional, and spiritual needs in the way I know best." Her plan is also to allow those needs to evolve as one step leads to another and to be open to these changing needs.

Louise's Plan B is a plan for the Solution-Oriented Life that will work for everyone. Anyone living an authentic life has found his or her solution. And no matter how difficult it is to achieve that solution, it becomes the only possible thing you can do. That solution will involve honesty, integrity, and excellence—but it will be honesty to *yourself*, integrity to your *own* values, and pursuing excellence on behalf of your *own* principles, not those of others.

Louise threw out her Plan A, which was to become whatever a person close to her wished her to be, in order to win their love. She chose a Plan B that opted for reciprocal relationships only—ones where she attracted people who admired the real Louise and not a fake one. *Becoming your real Self is the easiest way to live, because you use no extra energy to maintain a pretense*. The people who are attracted to you are attracted to your quietness or activity, your sense of humor or seriousness, as the case may be. No extra energy needs to be expended on your part to *pretend* to be an extrovert or *pretend* to be witty.

Think of how much energy you've spent over your lifetime pretending to be someone you're not, and you can see that once you stop living a false life, you'll have enough dynamism to move mountains. I've seen it happen over and over again. A dynamic life is one filled with meaningful activity and with no room for boredom or purposelessness. Since you'll be living a meaningful life, you'll eventually find a mission or cause you'll want to put your energy into and that cause will be one that you're enthusiastic about and devoted to. This mission could be raising a family, a vocation or hobby you wish to follow, or a volunteer activity you find important. *The best life is one where everything you do is part of your life's purpose and meaning.* That may sound serious, and it is, but the best part is *you'll have fun doing it.* And you find this life when you've conscientiously thought through your role, first with yourself, followed by family, community, and Creation itself.

For many people, searching for and finding their true Self comes from the hard work of sifting through accumulated layers of debris—from accepting other people's agendas when they're not the correct program for themselves. If you use the techniques of prioritizing, brainstorming, and so on, you'll probably see your way clear to arriving at the goal you wish to achieve. But what if you try as hard as you can and still see your way roadblocked? Roadblocks usually disappear as we throw aside the boulders of depression and low self-esteem that cause them. But every once in a while, those boulders are just too heavy for one person and need a helping hand.

Psychotherapy is that helping hand if you feel stuck in your problems and unable to reclaim your Authentic Self on your own. It can help you unpeel the layers that keep the person you truly are covered up and in the dark. Though a small part of the work you'll do in therapy may be painful as you go over distressing experiences, most of it becomes exhilarating as you begin to unwrap and discover the best present in the world—the gift of Yourself. Over and over, I've been struck by someone telling me how they recognize this first moment of feeling alert, alive, and happy as being "who they really are." They may have spent their entire lives feeling depressed, anxious, or blue, yet that fleeting moment is enough for them to recognize *this* person to be the true one and not that old, familiar individual they've known for so long.

Three years after Louise completed therapy, she contacted me and we met briefly. She was more vibrant than ever and the gains she made had had a permanent effect. The reaction her new friends had given her at that Christmas party long ago had enabled her to feel socially accepted for the first time. She became friendly with three or four women and one or two widowers, and they formed a group that went to movies, concerts, and restaurants together—though, she said laughingly, the widowers were platonic friends only and would remain that way.

Her two sons have gotten jobs and actually treat Louise in a more respectful manner than they had when they lived at home and Louise was busy trying to buy their love. She's still very involved in the orchestra, and music has become intensely meaningful to her. She also cooks meals once a week for a soup kitchen sponsored by her church. Louise had been a wonderful cook and had lavished delicious meals upon her sons and lover in an effort to express her talent and make them love her. Those meals were one more reason why no one left her. But now Louise said that making those simple recipes for the homeless gives her more joy than she ever had when cooking the more expensive and complicated dishes she lavished on her unappreciative diners.

When you reclaim yourself and implement solutions that lead you to your Authentic Self, you will find *you*, just as Louise did. You'll no longer wish to hold on to a Plan A that is keeping you locked in painful circumstances. Instead, you'll be exploring and implementing a Plan B that will help you reclaim your true Self. And then you can find joy.

# SOLUTIONS FOR RELATIONSHIPS:
## Communicating Honestly

Most people are either in a relationship or between relationships. It's good to be in a harmonious partnership, but is it okay to be in a mediocre or poor one just for the sake of being with someone? My answer is no. I don't mean that you should walk out of a so-so marriage just because it isn't fun anymore, or abandon a relationship that requires hard work and is difficult. I do mean that *most relationships that have become routine and many that have slipped into anger, frustration, and recriminations can be transformed into happy and intimate ones again.*

How do they get to that happy outcome? By learning how to resolve past hurts and anger and then learning to form a Plan B that provides for *both* their needs to be met. They've learned in their counseling sessions that a Plan B for couples must be a *mutual* plan.

Take the following quiz to see how you're getting along in your most important relationship right now:

## HOW HAPPY IS YOUR RELATIONSHIP?

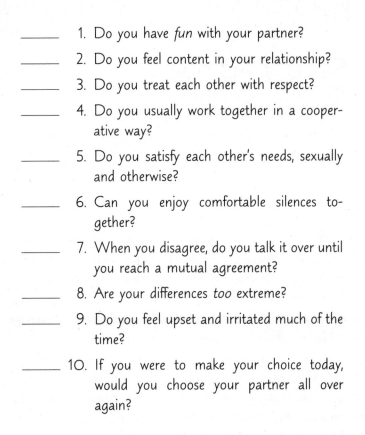

_____  1. Do you have *fun* with your partner?

_____  2. Do you feel content in your relationship?

_____  3. Do you treat each other with respect?

_____  4. Do you usually work together in a cooperative way?

_____  5. Do you satisfy each other's needs, sexually and otherwise?

_____  6. Can you enjoy comfortable silences together?

_____  7. When you disagree, do you talk it over until you reach a mutual agreement?

_____  8. Are your differences *too* extreme?

_____  9. Do you feel upset and irritated much of the time?

_____ 10. If you were to make your choice today, would you choose your partner all over again?

If you have a wonderful relationship that works, all of your answers will be Yes except for questions 8 and 9, where a No will be your response. Many couples will probably have one or two answers opposite to this ideal, but even one opposite answer means you can work to make your relationship better. A no answer to question 10 should make you think about the reason you wouldn't choose this same partner and whether it can be altered to make it better.

All relationships start with a Plan A that the partners agree to verbally, or more often, nonverbally. But, as we've seen, it's difficult enough for one person to make his or her Plan A work. How much more difficult it is then, for *two* people to have their dreams mesh exactly? Almost everyone enters relationships starry-eyed and fantasizing that their dreams will come true, but many later enter a state of disillusionment when that fantasy fails to happen.

When couples come to see me, the first thing I do is listen to them and help them decide whether there's any remnant left of the love they used to have for one another. *If there's a shred left, then the prognosis is good, no matter how angry they are at each other or how much their marriage or relationship has deteriorated.* What they need is a Plan B that satisfies not their fantasies, but the realities of who they really are, what they really want, and how they wish to live their lives while getting there.

The key that I've discovered that answers the question, "Can we save this relationship?" is "Do you love her?" and then, "Do you love him?" If the answer to these two questions is yes, then no matter how hard the partners have to work, that relationship can be not only saved, but greatly improved. If, on the other hand, I get answers like, "I really care about him," "I want the best for her," or "I love her like a sister or best friend," then unless that feeling can be changed to a more intense one, I've found there's not much glue to hold that couple together.

## COMMUNICATION

The long, slow slide from warm love and affection to indifference and antipathy is fueled not only by unfulfilled fantasies, but also by poor communication. *The foundation of a satisfying relationship is good communication skills. Good skills allow people to say true and difficult things to each other without getting angry and without their partner becoming angry.*

It's essential to say the truth to each other in order to improve your relationship. Besides passion, love is composed of respect and trust, and one or both of these is most often lacking when things go wrong. So regaining trust and respect is essential if you want to reestablish a healthy, harmonious relationship. Most relationships begin to go downhill when true feelings and emotions are withheld or when trivial issues are argued over and not the important, underlying ones. *To resolve problems and misunderstandings, it's essential to discuss the underlying issues rather than their many manifestations.* Addressing the underlying issue is the first step toward eliminating those countless moments of argument and bickering that drain so much energy and erode positive feelings. Most couples I see have spent months and years arguing over the sneeze and never treating the cold that causes it. Don't waste your time on the sneeze—cure the cold and the sneeze will automatically vanish.

Many people are afraid to confront their significant, underlying issues because they feel the marriage will explode, and then everything will be over. Nothing could be further from the truth. The major cause of arguments between couples occurs when their Plan A's don't mesh. Unless you learn to deal with divisive issues and arrive at a mutual Plan B, resentment will build up over time and eventually erode your relationship. Then, one day you'll wake up, look at your partner, and wonder why you're with this person at all. Good communication is telling each other the truth, but doing so in such a fashion that always shows respect to the other. And remember, respect is one of the key ingredients of love.

After attending a seminar with the late Dr. Penelope Russianoff, I developed four principles of communication that I have used in seminars and my private practice. When you learn and practice these four principles, you will be able to handle any situation well, *even if the other person is trying to be manipulative or abusive.*

Notice that I said *trying* to be manipulative or abusive. The way we speak is the way we think. Most people say, "She made me feel guilty," or "He made me do that." But if someone can *make* you do something, then you're powerless and a victim. So, you need to rephrase and say instead, "She *tried* to make me feel guilty," or "He *tried* to make me do that." Unfortunately, the rest of the sentence for many people is, ". . . and I let him" or ". . . and I let her."

When communication breaks down, anger is often the result. Although it's a new concept to most people, *no one is ever angry unless he or she feels powerless or like a victim. Unless someone is holding a gun to your head or a knife to your throat, no one can make you do anything.* The corollary to that statement is, if you realize a situation is making you feel victimized, refusing to accept that role means you no longer have to be angry. Any time you do, stop and think, "What about this situation is making me feel victimized?"

Once you understand that you *allow* people to make you feel guilty or make you do things you don't want to do, you can also see that you can *refuse to allow it* and take back control of your life. Then the corollary will be true—by refusing to buy into guilt or other manipulations, you won't be powerless anymore and you won't need to be angry.

*Understanding and practicing this life-changing principle can eliminate about 75 percent of the anger in your daily life.* Think back to any time in your life when you've been angry. Now try to think of any of those times when you haven't felt powerless, or like a victim. You can't, can you? *This means that if you learn how to communicate correctly and no longer play a victim role, you will never have to remain angry.* As soon as you feel a twinge of anger, you can teach yourself to stop, question what's happening to make you feel victimized, and then use the appropriate communication skills listed here to eliminate your powerlessness. This fresh concept of anger is so new to most people that you may have to ponder and rethink the way you've conducted all your relationships, including your current one.

## THE FOUR PRINCIPLES OF COMMUNICATION

I recommend that you write down these four rules on a small card and carry it with you for two weeks. If you use it faithfully for that period of time, you'll have formed a new habit that can transform your life.

## 1. You Have the Right to Speak Your Mind

Don't bother to state a desire or opinion to your spouse or partner unless and until you believe you have the right to say it. If you believe you have the right to state something, your tone of voice will be very different than if you *don't* believe you have that right. *Approximately 80 percent of what we convey in our speech is conveyed by tone of voice and not by the actual words.*

If you find this hard to believe—I know I did at first—try a little experiment. Say "The sky is blue" in a matter-of-fact tone of voice. It comes out as a simple statement, doesn't it? And when you listen to your tone of voice, you can see that others will hear it as a simple statement of fact also. Next, say the same sentence in a threatening tone. Though the words remain neutral, the sound of the sentence has a sinister, menacing quality, doesn't it? Now, say it again a third way—in a timid, questioning tone. How does that neutral sentence sound now? You can see by this little experiment how much tone of voice influences how we hear other people and how other people hear us.

The reason it's important to believe you have the right to say such things as, "I need you to behave more respectfully to me," or "I want you to include me in decisions that concern both of us," is that if you believe you have the right to make these statements, your tone of voice will be calm, level, and authoritative. People who know they're respected and hold positions of authority give others directions without screaming or getting angry. They *expect* their words to be heeded. Screaming and yelling is innately viewed as weakness, and others—men in particular—will often disregard the actual content of the statement. What's worse, they often disregard the person who's doing the screaming, and dismiss her as a "hysterical female" or a "crazy lady," and things get worse and worse. How can you arrive at a joint Plan B when your partner dismisses your words, thoughts, and needs?

In addition to the right to state a need that's important to you, *you also have the right to say no and the right to take time to think*. More people get in trouble by not heeding these rights than almost any other communication problems they encounter. When you've read all four rules, you'll see how you can be polite and still say no, and also how you can take time to think before you blurt out something you'll regret.

## 2. Formulate Your Statement Using "I" Rather Than "You" Language

You need to think of a statement that will express the complete communication you want to make to your partner, friend, boss, or colleague. Your statement should be short, sweet, and to the point. This will ensure that you don't put so many needs into your communication that your partner receives an unclear message and gets confused. People also tend to try *explaining* why they need what they're stating and end up sounding defensive to the other person.

Think of what you want your statement to be. Take all the time you need to do so. Tell your partner that you need to take time to think of your statement. Your tone of voice should be firm but calm and your voice should go down at the end of each sentence.

Let's suppose your partner or spouse is not as romantic as you'd like him or her to be. Number one, do you have the right to discuss it? Yes, you do. Next, what is the statement you'd like to say, using "I" rather than "You"? This takes a lot of thought but after a while you might come up with something such as, "I need you to do romantic things more often."

Compare that to what most people usually say: "Why don't you ever bring me flowers?" or "You never do anything romantic." *Do not use questions when trying to communicate something important.* It's much too easy to be off and running with such answers as, "What do you mean I don't bring you flowers? I brought you some a few months ago." Questions by their very nature cannot be statements, where you say something in a matter-of-fact tone of voice and your inflection goes down at the end of the sentence. Questions make your voice go *up* and leave it open for the other person to respond with a question also, such as "What do you mean by that?" and so on and on, with both parties getting angrier and angrier.

The second sentence, "You never do anything romantic," is wrong for two reasons. The first is, *don't make a "you" statement.* The other person will feel attacked and become defensive. Usually that means they do one of two things—they get angry, withdraw, and build a wall around themselves, or they attack back. Neither attack nor withdrawal makes for the calm communication that leads to understanding each other's wishes and needs. The second reason the statement is unhelpful is that "Always" or "Never" statements don't work because they're untruthful. Does he really *never* do anything romantic? Probably, he infrequently or very infrequently makes romantic gestures or says romantic things—at least, not as often as you'd like and appreciate. Does she *always* criticize you? Probably not always, but perhaps you feel she does so fairly often. Communication can succeed only when one person speaks truthful statements and the other replies truthfully. And when you and your partner speak truthfully to each other, trust and respect can grow—and trust and respect are the cornerstones of love. If one person speaks truthful statements and the other speaks manipulative ones, the first person can repeat his or her sentence and refuse to be sucked into the manipulation, and the truth will be restated.

Another reason "Always" and "Never" statements are harmful is that the other person senses they're not true— "I *do too* take out the garbage and I just did last Tuesday." Then your partner feels justified in rejecting *all* of your statement and, again, dismissing you in the process. It's much better to formulate your sentence, such as "We had an agreement that you would take out the garbage every evening and I need you to live up to that agreement." Can you hear the difference in feeling that sentence makes, compared with, "You never take out the garbage?" *Proper communication maintains good feeling and respect as difficult issues are worked out between two people who have real and important differences and interests.* You and your partner's Plan A's need to be peacefully exchanged so that they can be listened to, opted for, modified, or discarded for a mutual Plan B.

A very important point in communicating needs is not to make your spouse or partner feel trapped. A trapped person lashes out and fights, or goes along but is resentful. Very few people are really trapped, but perceive themselves to be. For instance, Beth told Jon they had been dating for eight months and that was long enough—it was time to get engaged. Jon felt trapped because he was not ready for marriage and not completely sure Beth was the woman he wanted to spend the rest of his life with. (He wasn't trapped at all since, in reality, he could have walked out the door, but he felt trapped by his own ambivalence and love for her.) His perception of being trapped became his reality, though, and he responded as if she really were binding him in chains.

Jon's sentence ought to have been, "I love you but I'm not ready for marriage yet." That's clear, but not what Beth hoped to hear. However, very few people respond with the sentence they *should* say. Many men in that situation will not speak clearly at all, yet continue to feel trapped. Of course, Jon could have ended the relationship, but he loved Beth and so he didn't. Instead they ended up in my office because he was ambivalent and resentful and was delivering mixed messages, and they argued constantly.

During counseling, Beth learned not to make Jon feel trapped. When she made "I" statements, her statements reflected her own needs and weren't perceived as orders to Jon. Her statement became, "I love you and want to marry you. I know you love me too, but you may not be ready for marriage yet. I want to get married soon, so I need an answer from you. If you don't want to get married now, I need to break up with you so I can date and find someone who wants to build a life and family with me. But you may not want to do that. Why don't you take a few weeks and think it over, and whatever your decision is will be OK— we'll both know where we stand. Will two weeks be enough time to decide?" (These sentences seem a little stilted but they very clearly state what Beth thinks. Once you learn how to communicate correctly, your sentences will become more natural, but meanwhile, it's OK to have them sound a little awkward.)

Beth asked Jon for a two-week hiatus in their relationship, to give him time to respond to her need for a commitment. If Jon had been unable to give a firm yes or no answer at the end of that time, then Beth could have asked for a three-month break. When the three-month break takes place, there is no contact, and therefore no negotiation, but it comes *after* it's clear your plans don't match and you can't formulate a joint plan.

Beth's Plan A was to marry Jon. Jon's Plan A was to continue to date Beth with no specific blueprint for their future. Beth's statement made clear she wanted Jon to accept her plan, but only if he could do so wholeheartedly and without duress. She would proceed with Plan B if necessary, but she preferred her Plan A. She was also clear that she would not accept Jon's Plan A—that was out of the question for her.

Beth's words and tone of voice conveyed to Jon that she really meant what she said, but since *he* was the one to make the decision, Jon no longer felt trapped. Once that occurred, he scheduled some individual sessions to talk over his fears and feelings and was able to resolve his ambivalence. He found the positives outweighed the negatives and, faced with losing Beth, he was able to commit to marriage with her. Because it really *was* his decision, his resentment of her "making" him marry her evaporated, and the issue was happily resolved.

Note that what Beth communicated to Jon was difficult for him to hear. He didn't want to make a decision immediately, and didn't like it; yet her clear communication cleared the way for a resolution of their impasse. Jon could have responded that he wasn't ready for marriage and couldn't commit himself to it, and then Beth would have been the one to receive a message she didn't want to hear. But that too, would have been valuable to her because it would have enabled her to get on with her Plan B—a married life with a family. Good communication is the only way to clear away the debris of a relationship, make room for more positive feelings and sympathies, or face the fact that no joint Plan B is possible.

## 3. Repeat, Repeat, Repeat

This principle means that when someone changes the subject, goes off on a tangent, or tries a manipulative answer (notice I said *tries*) you answer him or her and then *repeat your original sentence*, either exactly or in a paraphrased manner. For instance, if your sentence is "I need you to remember my birthday with a gift" and the response is "I did give you a gift," repeat yourself and say, "You gave me a gift two years ago but I need you to give me a gift every single birthday." Messages become plain and more clarified as the conversation continues.

Couples, families, old friends, and business colleagues know each other's Achilles' heel. They know so well how to push each other's buttons and do so much of the time, especially when relationships are dysfunctional or need improvement. For example, Jane used to schedule disagreeable chores for her husband, Carl, just on those nights when she knew he wanted to go out with his friends. Instead, using these new principles of communication, she learned to say, "I need you to spend more time with me and not go out with the 'boys' three nights a week" (notice how specific her statement is). However, he did not respond with "OK" and never go out with them again! Unfortunately, this scenario will never happen.

*This is so because people have patterns in relationships, and no one established in a relationship with someone else will give up his or her familiar pattern after only one interaction.* A person who can't keep his or her Plan A the first time around will try to do so a second and third time by using another approach. This is especially true in manipulative or dysfunctional relationships. Let's see how this works and how Repeating helps you reply appropriately, no matter what response you're given.

Jane finally believes she has (1) *the right* to ask Carl to stay home with her more and not go out with the guys three nights a week. Because she believes she has this right, she can (2) *formulate her sentence using an "I" statement* and calmly ask him to do so. Notice the difference between "I need you to spend more time with me and not go out with the 'boys' three nights a week" and "You never stay home with me. You always go out with the guys." You can see how the first sentence would make Carl think about the statement and the second would make him angry and defensive and lead nowhere except to a rousing argument.

But even if the first sentence made Carl thoughtful, there's no way he'll give in to Jane's request and stop going out. His answer might be, "I need to go out. I need some diversion after a hard day's work." Jane's old answer might have been, "So do I. What do you think I do all day? Sit on the sofa and eat bonbons?" But her new answer using the Repeating technique will be, "I work hard too, and I need your companionship in the evening."

Notice that's the end of the statement. She doesn't go on and on. Listen to how that would sound. "I work hard too, and I need your companionship in the evening. I come home after a hard day's work too, and then I make supper and then I do the dishes." Can you hear how going on too long takes the strength out of the statement and makes it sound weaker and more defensive? If Jane keeps quiet after she makes her statement, whether it's the first time or she's using Repeating and this is the second or third reply, Carl will hear her much more strongly because her statements are *short, sweet, and to the point.*

How many times does Repeating need to be used? *No one ever stops after the first time. They usually don't stop after the second time. They sometimes stop after the third time and they almost* always *stop after the fourth time.* There's just nowhere else to go. Let's run through Jane and Carl's entire interaction so you can get a sense of what happens and how Carl feels stopped in his ability to justify going out three nights a week, leaving Jane home alone.

JANE: "I need you to spend more time with me and not go out with the 'boys' three nights a week." (1x)

CARL: "I need to go out. I need some diversion after a hard day's work." (His Plan A was not to be out with friends, as Jane thought, but to get out and have fun. His answer, which Jane *listened to*, prevented them from going off on a tangent, and not resolving the real issue—change and diversion.)

JANE: "I work hard too and I need your companionship in the evening." (2x) (Her Plan A is articulated as needing Carl's time and companionship but not necessarily curtailing his fun.)

CARL: "Well, I want to go out and I need to." (Reiterates his Plan A.)

JANE: "I need to see more of you." (3x) "I need you to go out with your friends only once a week." (A change to Plan B—Carl would go out only once a week.)

CARL: "That won't work. I need to get out more than that." (Repeats his Plan A. States it for the third time.)

JANE: "I need to see more of you." (4x) "What if you go out with the guys once a week, and we go out together once or twice? Then I'd see more of you, you'd get out of the house, and I'd have more of your companionship." (Keeps her Plan B but enlarges it so that it can please him also, which is what makes a joint Plan B successful.)

CARL: "I'm not sure I'll be happy with that but we can give it a try." (He doesn't come up with another Plan B but agrees to try hers.)

JANE: "OK. Let's try it out and see if it works." (Agreement to try the amplified Plan B with the implication to talk again if necessary.)

Notice how Repeating works. Your partner's answer is always listened to and acknowledged. It's only *after* you've acknowledged the answer that you return to your original sentence and repeat or paraphrase it. If you just repeated your sentence over and over, you'd sound like a parrot and your partner might tune you out in annoyance. What happens when you listen to your partner's reply and answer it is that you give the other person the dignity of listening carefully, and both of you the opportunity to arrive at a mutual plan. Listening to responses is woefully lacking in many relationships—everyone clamors to be heard but no one's listening to what's said. And then there's no possible way to satisfy each other's needs.

## 4. "What's the Solution?"

Notice that Jane's two last statements contained possible solutions to their differing needs—she looked for Plan B. *The whole point of good communication is to find solutions to problems between you. It is not to win the argument and score points.* Because Carl was also using Repeating to stick to his statement—that he needed to get out and have fun—Jane introduced the fourth principle, "What's the Solution?," by suggesting they incorporate their needs into an answer that would satisfy them both.

Either person can and should introduce the concept of problem solving as soon as it becomes clear that (1) their needs differ and (2) a new interaction needs to replace the one they're arguing over. It doesn't matter who broaches the question—the first one who becomes aware that Plan B is needed is the one who should speak. Other variations of "What's the Solution?" are, "So what are we going to do about it?" "What's the answer?" "What can we do to solve this problem?" or "What's the Third Way?" Remember, your Plan A is the first way, your partner's is the second, and Plan B, jointly arrived at, is the Third Way.

The exchange between Jane and Carl went smoothly, with both parties speaking truthfully, yet without anger. *Good communication eliminates or vastly reduces anger, since neither person feels powerless or like a victim.* Both state what they think and feel until they arrive at a solution that will solve their problems. And both learn there's no need for anger, since they'll continue to communicate until they arrive at a mutually satisfying Plan B.

As you and your partner get better and better at arriving at a Solution-Oriented Life, your relationship will grow closer and more intimate. The anger and discontent that divided you will begin to disappear and, best of all, a new spirit will enter your life together—the feeling of optimism and a sense that things can continue to improve in the future. You'll have the tools to resolve issue after issue, and your marriage can return from a mediocre condition, or worse, to the compatible, forward-looking state you originally shared.

Good communication is not only what you say to your partner. *It consists of the messages you give yourself.* It's so important to say "I let him make me feel guilty" rather than "He made me feel guilty." If your partner can *make* you feel guilty, you're powerless and in his control. If you think, "She's making me do this," you're her victim and have no control. But if you say to yourself, "She's trying to make me do this and I can either let her or decide not to," you've taken back control over your own life. You now have power again, even if it's only the power to sit and think about what Plan B might be.

I'm emphasizing this point because taking on the victim role and waiting for the other person to change is one of the foremost causes of marital misery. The victim feels powerless to change their spouse's behavior. It is correct that we can never change another person; we can only change ourselves. But because the spouse is *causing* the problem (having extramarital affairs, gambling, being abusive), it's natural for the victim to expect change to come from the *other* person.

The problem is that the offending spouse doesn't want change and won't come for help, so I end up seeing the partner who's been victimized. What I've found over and over again is that when the *victim* changes and decides to take responsibility for his or her own life, the old pattern is broken and then things must change.

## Breaking an Abusive Pattern

Chip was a pharmacist in his early 30s who'd become angrier over the ten-year span of his marriage. As life became more stressful and there was more financial pressure and more noise in the house from their two sons, Chip began to hit and punch Diana. The first time he did this, she was so shocked that she didn't know how to react. Chip was shocked too, felt terribly guilty, and promised never to do it again.

But he did, and the usual pattern of spousal abuse developed, aided by *both* parties. Chip's stress level would rise and tension would build, but it would release itself when he beat Diana. Remorse would follow; Diana would be hurt and angry but would eventually succumb to the flowers, gifts, and promises Chip would make; there'd be a honeymoon period for a few weeks; and then the pattern would repeat itself.

When Diana came to see me, she was a sorry sight. There were no visible bruises, but she looked bedraggled and wan. Unlike other women I've seen in her situation, Diana didn't come from a home where there'd been abuse. She was hard on herself because she knew she shouldn't tolerate Chip's behavior or believe his promises any longer. One of Diana's problems was that she had left a job as store manager at the nearby mall in order to stay home with their two children, one an infant. Without an independent income, she felt powerless to even entertain the thought of leaving the marriage. And leaving a marriage with very young children is always an extremely difficult thing to do.

Diana's Plan A was to have a happy marriage with Chip and bring up their children in the pleasant house they'd bought two years ago. She had to acknowledge that Plan A wasn't working and no longer even existed. It had been in Meltdown for the last two or three years, and counseling and support helped her admit that to herself. Her internal message then became, "I need to make a plan for the future." Note that Diana's Plan B was just to formulate a plan. At this point, she couldn't conceive of what that plan might be.

At that moment, Diana took back control of her life. Even though most abused people need many months to figure out and implement a plan, Diana knew she would figure something out that could work and later, with the help of counseling, follow through on that plan, taking it step by step. She was finally taking responsibility for herself and her two young boys, and initiating action instead of living a life of reaction. She followed the four rules of good communication *to herself*, not to Chip, as she realized she had the right not to be abused. She then could formulate a sentence to herself, which was that same, simple statement—"I have the right not to be abused."

While Diana was in therapy, she also attended a group for abused spouses at the local Y. These groups are very valuable, and I recommend them heartily to people suffering verbal, emotional, or physical abuse in their marriage or relationship. Abusers try to isolate the victim, and group sessions bring the abused person back into a community of supportive people. The combination of attending group meetings while in individual therapy is a very powerful al-

liance and speeds up the recovery process necessary to deal
with the abuse. Diana decided in her heart that she would
never be hit by Chip again.

One day, as he began to move toward her in the threatening manner she knew all too well, Diana quietly told him
that if he ever touched her again, she would leave and divorce him. Something in her manner stopped Chip in his
tracks. The firm but quiet way she spoke told him she
meant it. Formerly, she would scream and cry when his
anger escalated and Chip always ignored it and went on to
beat her. This time something was different.

Diana announced that she would leave Chip if he didn't
get help and deal with his abuse. She told him he might
decide to do so or might decide not to, but what she needed
from this marriage was a husband who learned how to deal
with his own stress and not take it out on her. The power
equation between them changed immediately. Previously,
Chip had all the power and controlled Diana by his bullying rages. When Diana made the statement that she
would no longer stay around and perpetuate this arrangement, the power equation immediately changed.

*The victim gradually comes to understand that he or she is
part of an equation, and when one aspect of the equation changes,
the other aspect has to change also.* Whether your present relationship is good or bad, *you* are part of any equation involving yourself and another person.

Here are two examples that can help make this clear. If
Diana always responds to Chip's bullying (let's call that
response X) and Chip then beats her (response Y), then X
and Y become a stable pattern and can go on and on in

this manner. But once Diana, the victim in this situation, responds with a different response (let's call it Z), then Chip's Y no longer works. If he beat her again, she'd leave; therefore, he can't beat her again and still have his marriage. *So the victims in most situations have much more power than they ever realized they had.* They, not their "powerful" partner, have all the power they need, once they *recognize* they have it and that they can actually use it.

Diana's Plan B, which had been "I have the right not to be abused," was enlarged to become "I will stay in this marriage if I have a say and won't be abused. If not, I'll leave it." Almost everyone in an abusive relationship needs help and support to formulate a Plan B. The abused person comes to believe in the worthlessness the abuser tries to instill in him or her. An essential part of any psychotherapy or group counseling is to help the abused partner feel worthwhile again. Without that belief, change becomes impossible, but as the abused person begins to use good communication *to herself,* a feeling of self-worth can begin to grow and she can devise a Plan B. Then her victimhood can finally be laid aside.

## MAINTAINING A BALANCE OF POWER

Abusive relationships are about power and control, so it seems natural to think that good relationships should not be about these issues. But good relationships actually have a *balance* of power that has been worked out over the duration of the partnership. Usually this is an unconscious or semiconscious process that is negotiated between the two parties as differences arise. For instance, if Dee and Dennis are newlyweds and Dennis controls the checkbook and wants Dee to ask him for every penny, she can either acquiesce and hand over power and control to Dennis or she can make a stand, declare their marriage a partnership, and ask for equal rights in their relationship.

It's important for people not *just* to take a stand, but to accommodate the foibles and weaknesses of each partner, and good marriages do so. For instance, Dennis may want to control the money because they both agree Dee is a spendthrift. Or, he may want control because he's afraid of losing power completely in the relationship, as he saw his father do. They need to arrive at a carefully negotiated Plan B where their strengths and weaknesses are dealt with in a manner that enables their marriage to be fair, yet survive in a healthy manner. In good relationships, issues are resolved so that each person handles the matters he or she excels in and helps to compensate for the other's weaknesses. Plan B's are arrived at by these negotiations, and that's why it's so important for partners to be fairly equal in power. After Dennis and Dee resolved the money issue, Dee said, "When you meet someone fifty-fifty, it's not reporting, it's sharing."

It's easy to see the need for a balance of power by looking at how labor and management negotiate new contracts. If labor has all the power, management will have to give workers too many benefits and the company will not be able to compete with rival corporations. On the other hand, if management has all the power, they can refuse benefits and wage increases and the workers will lose out. The best negotiations are conducted when labor and management are fairly equal, and then good collective bargaining—an excellent phrase—can take place. Labor has a Plan A they're (secretly) willing to modify, so does management, and a joint Plan B is arrived at that leaves the workplace running smoothly for years.

In the same manner, when couples are trying to negotiate important issues, hard bargaining usually takes place. If good communication principles are used, it can be done intensely, but without anger. It's when one of the parties feels unequal in the negotiation process that resentment and hard feelings develop. Remember that in almost every circumstance, no matter how difficult, you are probably *not* a victim and are *not* trapped. Developing and stating a Plan B, first to yourself and then to your partner, will increase your power and eliminate the anger, resentment, and bitterness that poison relationships in which one partner is perceived as having all the control. And just like the union contract, happy marriages result when the partners discuss and negotiate major issues and agree upon a mutual Plan B. Then daily life can go smoothly, with all major disagreements dealt with and out of the way. In good marriages, power is never an issue on a daily basis, but emerges only with conflict, and then is used in the service of finding a new Plan B.

The more disagreements eliminated between you and your partner, the more psychological and emotional room you have for compatibility and good times to return. If your emotional space is junked up with marital debris, it uses up room necessary to let those good times in. The more you clean up your emotional attic, the more you'll be able to live the Solution-Oriented Life that will bring you and your spouse the happiness you desire.

Just as union contracts need to be renegotiated every few years, so too does your own partnership agreement. If you're married, you signed a written marriage contract at your wedding, but all partnerships and marriages have an unwritten contract also—we're just usually not fully aware of what it is. None of us remain the same as we age from 18 to 80; we never stop changing, but it may happen so slowly that we only recognize it when something seems out of synch. When something does feel wrong in your marriage and you realize that you're angry or frustrated with your partner, instead of venting that anger or frustration, stop and think, "What is *really* going on?" Remember, one of your rights is the right to take time to think. You may realize that you've entered a different stage of life and you need to change something about yourself or something in your partnership agreement. You may be stuck in a Plan B you both agreed upon that has worked for years, but the circumstances of your life may have changed, and therefore your needs also.

Common factors that change are becoming a parent, starting or ending work, relocation, aging, family illness, or just graduating from your 20s to your 30s and so on. Many of these factors are sudden and immediately recognized, but others creep up so slowly that you may only recognize their occurrence in hindsight. I have a saying I've found especially true of many women: "Some people are 18 until they're 35." When I use that phrase to someone I'm seeing, it usually gets instant recognition and they say, "That's me." One 30-year-old woman recently laughed and answered, "But I'm not even 18 yet!" I think this concept is true because many people—women, especially—have been brought up to please and go along with roles that were handed to them. But at some point, often in their 30s, they realize they've spent their lives living someone else's Plan A and have no plan of their own.

A new Plan B must be devised for all these changing factors. Your inner or outer reality has changed and your goals, dreams, and visions may need to be altered or changed also. First, you must look inside yourself, understand your new needs, and then communicate them to your spouse. This may prompt your partner to assess the shifts occurring in his or her own life. Once you discuss these changes, you can form a Plan B that gives you mutual satisfaction for your current circumstances. And if you and your partner haven't practiced good communication in the past, this may be your chance to develop a joint Plan B for the very first time.

When you develop your joint Plan B or update outmoded or outworn plans using the four principles of communication, you'll arrive at the place your relationship *should* be at this moment. Some couples may sadly agree that their visions and dreams have grown too different and their Plan B's can never merge. But most couples will find that their marriage or relationship isn't a mediocre state to be tolerated, but a vibrant, joyous way to travel through time together. I can tell you from twenty-five years of seeing couples resolve their problems and achieve a happy, Solution-Oriented marriage that you probably can do so too. And the energy you'll use to get there is much less than the energy you'll consume by argument and dissension. I urge you to give it all you've got. It will get you to where you want to be—living in a relationship that's happy, compatible, and mutually fulfilling.

# SOLUTIONS FOR FAMILIES: Making Order out of Chaos

Families nourish us and provide refuge and safety from the world, but they are also the instruments that most often make us crazy and distort our lives. Family members know each other so well that each person knows how to push the others' buttons—and in many cases, they often do.

Your family—the one you live in now, or your family of origin—may function in a loving and supportive manner most of the time. Or you may have a family that's totally dysfunctional. But if you're like most people, your family will sometimes make you feel wonderful and at other times drive you to distraction. This chapter will discuss some common problems people encounter with their families, so you can learn how finding solutions will preserve your sanity and eliminate frustration and anger.

All of us want the calm, peace, and harmony that come from living a sane family life. So what is it about many families that makes their members feel *insane* whenever they interact? Over the years, I've come to believe that in the best of families, patterns that sometimes formed due to circumstance have become embedded, so that each member learns a stereotypical response to the others that prevents expressing a full range of emotions and behavior.

We're all meant to be complete human beings, capable of reacting to differing events with an entire repertoire of emotional and behavioral responses. The more responses we come up with in new situations, the more survival capability we possess. But when families are dysfunctional, members are stuck both in their own *individual* roles and in an unchanging, *interactive* response to the other family members. A good definition of dysfunction is one where family members deal with stresses using stereotyped interactions that not only leave problems unresolved, but actually enable them to continue. The healthy survival of that family and each of its members begins to erode, and a less vital and flexible unit is left to deal with the inevitable ups and downs of daily life.

## PROBLEM SOLVING IN THE FAMILY

The following quiz will help you see how much of your own family life is spent in ways that lead to problems and not to solutions:

_____ 1. When you experience difficulty, do you approach your family with an expectation that you'll get help and support?

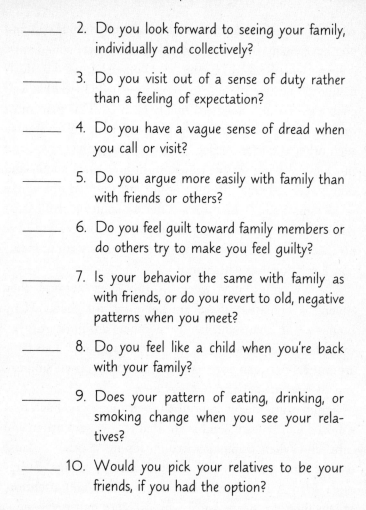

_____ 2. Do you look forward to seeing your family, individually and collectively?

_____ 3. Do you visit out of a sense of duty rather than a feeling of expectation?

_____ 4. Do you have a vague sense of dread when you call or visit?

_____ 5. Do you argue more easily with family than with friends or others?

_____ 6. Do you feel guilt toward family members or do others try to make you feel guilty?

_____ 7. Is your behavior the same with family as with friends, or do you revert to old, negative patterns when you meet?

_____ 8. Do you feel like a child when you're back with your family?

_____ 9. Does your pattern of eating, drinking, or smoking change when you see your relatives?

_____ 10. Would you pick your relatives to be your friends, if you had the option?

Congratulations if you answered yes to questions 1, 2, 7, and 10 and no to questions 3, 4, 5, 6, 8, and 9—you have a wonderful, mature family relationship. However, if you're like many people, you'll probably have one or two different responses to these questions—and Chapter Seven will help you find solutions to achieve a better family life. If you find you have many opposite answers to this quiz, your family is living with Broken Dreams, and you either need to drastically alter your Plan A, or you need a Plan B that will enable everyone's needs to finally be met. This plan must include factors that will help you and your relatives give each other the love, respect, and trust everyone craves, and this may look impossible to you right now since people and events seem so crazy. But the Solution-Oriented Life works in *all* situations. It may be a different solution from what you envisioned, but when you find Plan B, others will have no choice but to be sane also—that is, if they want to maintain a relationship with you.

Most families stay stuck in problems because they haven't a clue that there are solutions for them. Many homes are in chaos and family members are in despair because they feel that "that's the way things are." The same arguments between parents and children, spouses, siblings, and in-laws are repeated *ad nauseam*.

Families are meant to nourish their members. Each person in a family wants and is entitled to love, attention, and care, and when things go wrong, it's most often because one or more relatives feel cheated of these things. Everyone's Plan A in a family is to receive love and attention. When they do, peace and harmony reign and everyone is able to enjoy each other and have fun together. All members feel secure and know they can get the help and support they need in good times and bad.

So when family members snipe and are sarcastic, scream and yell, or don't speak to each other for long periods of time, they feel their own Plan A is not being addressed. *People scream when they feel they're not being heard. If you're a screamer or you're being screamed at, you or the other person feels no one is listening.* If there's a lot of yelling at your house or when you get together with relatives, realize that somebody feels their needs are not being paid attention to. Once you understand this, you can begin to have a true conversation and ask, "What's really wrong?"—which is a question that asks for a solution to your problems.

In Chapter Six, you learned how to communicate your needs to one important person in your life. In a family, since there are many needs and points of view, communication may seem more complicated. Yet, the basic principles remain the same. If your plan is to gain love, respect, support, and trust from family members, you will still (1) believe you have the right to ask for these things; (2) formulate the statement that will express this need, using "I" instead of "You" statements; (3) Repeat, Repeat, Repeat; and (4) ask, "How can we resolve this?"

What makes resolving family problems different from resolving couple issues is that families seem to have an even greater stake in maintaining the status quo. In many families, everyone has a specific role. One is the smart one, another the athlete, another the pretty one, another the baby, and so on. This is beneficial up to a point, because it enables everyone to shine in a special area and be unique, but it also chokes off the full range of abilities and emotions all people need to develop. When the pretty one ages, the athlete stops competing, or the baby grows up, that person's limited role leads to feelings of failure and loss of esteem. With only one role fully developed, adult behavior isn't acquired.

People who are stuck in a stereotypical role make up a large percentage of my practice. Their families did not provide a playing field where different roles could be explored, mistakes made, small steps praised, and conflicts resolved. Instead, rigid roles and stereotypical behavior were rewarded—so they didn't know how to act and react with others in their adult lives, and they got themselves into trouble.

The extreme of this situation is found in alcoholic families. One child may be the peacemaker, another the surrogate parent, another the scapegoat, and yet another the inadequate one. Very often, the child chosen as the peacemaker is expected to perform this impossible task from a very young age. Since no child can possibly stop her parents from fighting, the burden becomes too heavy and feelings of guilt and failure result when she can't succeed. This role and these feelings will follow her into her own adult life.

This is what happened to Amanda, who came to see me when she realized she was trying to rescue everyone in her life, and was going under in the process. Her mother had been an alcoholic ever since Amanda could remember, and her father had retreated to his workbench from the chaos in their home. As the oldest of five children (often the peacemaker and surrogate-parent role is assigned to the oldest), Amanda effectively took over the mother role: cleaning, cooking, disciplining the younger children, and trying to keep family life going.

Though Amanda lost years of her childhood to this burdensome role, the household tasks were actually easier to accomplish than the emotional ones. She tried to keep the younger children from fighting in order to let her mother sleep all day. She tried to placate her mother when she was screaming in a drunken rage. When she failed, she felt inadequate, resentful, and guilty. Then, when she wasn't successful, her mother would punish her with the silent treatment and Amanda would twist herself inside out in order to get her mother to speak to her again. These silences could go on for a week or two, and during that time her mother would pass messages to her through the other children.

At 32, Amanda found herself with Bob, her alcoholic husband who couldn't hold a job, and two little children whom she left in day care while she worked as a nurse in the local hospital. It's extremely common for adult children of alcoholics to either become alcoholics themselves or marry someone who is. Amanda did the latter and spent the seven years of their marriage continuing her peacemaker role and running interference for her husband, just as she had done in her original family. She made excuses to his boss for absences when he had a hangover, admitted guilt for crimes she did not commit in order to quiet his rages, and thrust herself physically and emotionally between him and their children so they wouldn't be beaten.

In addition, Amanda attracted friends who had multiple problems and who leaned on her for help. They were clinging and dependent and made Amanda feel, as she put it, "sucked dry." Her mother was still drinking, her father was still passive, and her siblings still counted on her to play the mother role for all the scrapes they were constantly involved in. These ranged from minor infractions with the law to using drugs and alcohol and inadequacy in handling life's daily problems. Amanda was the healthy one, the strong one, and she fulfilled her role as of old. Of course, she could no more fix these problems as an adult than she could as a child; she ended up strong on the outside but feeling on the inside as if she were cracking in two.

Amanda had been attending ACOA (Adult Children of Alcoholics) meetings for six months before she entered my office, and had finally come to the conclusion that *she* was the one who needed changing, not the others. Obviously, they needed to change also, but she finally recognized that she was totally powerless to make them do so.

Her Plan A, both in childhood and adult life, was to take care of everyone's problems and make things work. She'd been rewarded when they did and punished when they didn't. That's how we all learn, and Amanda was an apt pupil. She'd learned her lessons so well that she was bogged down by rescuing her husband, parents, and siblings long after it was harmful to everyone involved to do so. She agreed that her Plan A—to fix everyone's problems—had to be discarded. Yet she was very reluctant to give up her role as peacemaker and parental figure.

When people want to change, they have to confront not only the anger they'll get from family members who want them to continue in old patterns, but even more, their own reluctance to give up their familiar role. Amanda had al- ways gained whatever self-esteem she had from the knowledge that it was she who was keeping her family together. If she gave up that role, who would she be and what would she do? Her identity was so tied up in her *limited* role that she couldn't conceive of a more complete one. This is true of most people at a certain stage in therapy—they've given up the old role that no longer works, but they can't quite foresee the new one, so for a while they feel as if they're in limbo.

It took some time for her to understand that her only role was to be *Amanda*, and our job was to discover who that really was. I told her that in all my years of practice, when people discover who they really are, they find a unique and beautiful person whom they may be meeting for the very first time. Amanda didn't believe me at first, as so many people don't. They're so full of depressed and angry feelings that they don't feel beautiful at all and can't conceive it's possible to be so.

As Amanda continued in therapy, she developed a Plan B that she phrased as "I will take care of my own needs and the *legitimate* needs of others. I expect all my relationships to be reciprocal, and I'll no longer spend most of my time and energy doing things for people that they should be doing for themselves."

She told her husband that he was free to drink or to stop drinking, but she would file for divorce if he chose not to go to AA and stay sober. Because of her calm, firm tone of voice, he heard her message loud and clear. After grumbling and telling her to leave if she wanted to, he began to attend meetings and eventually stopped drinking. Next, she refused to take her mother's calls when her mother was drunk and argumentative. Amanda's mother didn't stop drinking, but learned to phone on weekend mornings when she was relatively sober.

When Amanda refused to bail out her brothers and sisters any longer, they were angry and told her how much nicer she'd been before she went into therapy. That's when Amanda knew she was making progress. She told them that helping them had depleted her emotionally and financially, but had also deprived *them* of learning how to resolve problems, the hallmark of an adult human being.

Amanda was under enormous pressure from all her relatives to remain in her old role. Alcoholic families are extremely manipulative and they pull out all the stops to try to keep family members from changing. Because Amanda wanted and needed the Plan B of a happy, productive life, her family wasn't able to keep her in the role of rescuer.

In less than a year, Amanda was transformed from a depressed, angry, worn-out young woman to a confident person sure of her self-worth and looking forward to the future. She wasn't exactly sure what that future would hold, but now that she was taking good care of herself and helping with only the legitimate needs of others, she had more time and energy to make good choices for her life. Notice that even *before* she was sure of her plan, Amanda had renewed confidence and self-esteem. No one has to wait for Plan B to be fully operational in order to feel happier and more vibrant. Hope and self-confidence born of a realistic plan and small successes are enough to begin living the Solution-Oriented Life.

As Amanda began putting Plan B into practice, the first

thing she noticed was how much space there was for so many other things she'd always wanted to do. You too, will find physical and emotional time and energy to pursue positive goals when you find a Plan B that encompasses *your* needs *as well as* those of others.

Amanda rejected forever the Plan A she'd been taught as a child—"My role is to take care of others' needs, whether possible or not, and no matter how much it depletes my physical or emotional health"—and live by the Plan B of "taking good care of myself and the legitimate needs of others who are close to me in a reciprocal relationship." If you've been elected as the caretaker in a family where others don't pull their weight, consider Amanda's Plan B and whether or not it might work for you.

## ADJUSTING THE SIZE OF YOUR BUNDLE

Agnes Sanford was a writer of books on spirituality and a great healer. So many people asked her to pray for them that she felt depleted, inadequate, and drained. Finally, an idea came to her that allowed her to discern whom she could help and whom she couldn't. What occurred to her was that she should only help people who were "in her bundle." That's an unusual phrase, yet instantly understandable. What happens if you're taking on the caretaker and peacemaker roles is that everyone and everything becomes your bundle and you feel as if you're sinking under the weight—*which you are*. It's sometimes difficult to realize exactly what's wrong—it seems something's wrong with *you.* You've always been the strong one, yet you feel weak and incapable. If this is your problem, your Plan B must include determining who's in your bundle and who isn't—and what's in your bundle and what isn't. *The whole world is not in your bundle.*

*You* are always in your bundle. The person who's been lost in all those years of caretaking is *yourself.* Many of the people I see think that taking care of their own legitimate needs is selfish. They were told that as children, and their relatives continue to repeat it every time they try to move toward health. If this is true of you, your first task will be to *learn the difference between selfishness and taking good care of yourself.* My own belief is that we're here on earth for a reason—we can't always figure out just what that reason is—so, while we're here, we need to nurture ourselves using the same standards we'd use for our own children. You must learn how to become your own parent and treat yourself as if you were your own beloved child.

What are those standards? *To provide for your own legitimate needs and the legitimate needs of those in your bundle.* While your needs may differ from those around you and even vary for yourself at differing times in your life, you always have the legitimate need for food, clothing, shelter, love, support, and becoming your true Self. Becoming your true Self never means becoming a selfish person—that is no one's true Self, but a distortion that disappears as you find solutions to your life and become the authentic person you were meant to be.

Amanda's marriage improved when Bob became sober and continued in AA. Some of the people I see don't have that good fortune and eventually choose divorce. Her mother didn't stop drinking, but Amanda no longer tried "fixing" that and became comfortable with a more limited relationship. The children saw their grandmother only when she was sober, and Amanda no longer heard her scream. Her brothers and sisters ceased calling when she stopped bailing them out of their innumerable scrapes, but that was also all right, as Amanda refused to buy their love any longer.

Amanda decided that if the only reason her family was interested in her was because of what she gave them, instead of being interested in her *for herself*, she would no longer be involved in those relationships. She told each of her siblings that she cared for them and wanted a good relationship with them but would no longer buy their love. Her Plan B of taking good care of herself and wanting reciprocal, legitimate family ties, which by now she believed in passionately, wouldn't allow it. But she left the door open for them to approach her in the future if they ever wished to resume a healthy relationship.

People who care about themselves won't hang around to take abuse from others, no matter how close those family members may be. But while they refuse to continue in old, manipulative interactions, they often invite their family to call or write *when that family member becomes ready for a new, healthy pattern*. The door is left open, boundaries are set, and the statement can be made lovingly. For instance, Amanda said to her siblings, "I love you because you're my brothers and sisters but I feel you've taken advantage of me and not worked out your problems on your own. I can't continue in this way anymore, but if you're ever ready to see me just for family get-togethers, please call. I'd love to get together in that way."

The advantage of this statement is that Amanda doesn't have to worry and wonder about getting in touch with her family and what's going on in their lives. She decided she couldn't continue in that old, stressful way. So she goes about her life not dwelling on the hurt and pain, and, hopefully, one day, she'll receive a pleasant phone call. But she may not. The ball is in their court.

*Always leave the ball in the other person's court.* You've probably spent much of your life running around holding a ball you didn't know what to do with. But if you make a centered statement of what you truly believe, the other person has to respond to *you*, and that's the way it should be. Another example from Amanda's life to illustrate this concept is her statement to Bob to "quit drinking and get in a program or I'm filing for divorce." She'd been tremendously upset about his drinking and abuse, but once she came to Plan B—that he could make whatever choice he wished, but she would stay in the marriage only if he chose health—the ball was in Bob's court and Amanda felt much calmer.

Alcoholism is by no means the only problem that can cause chaos and distortion in families. Infidelity, drugs, inordinate debt, out-of-control kids, arguing in all its various forms, and verbal, emotional, and physical abuse cause the same type of problems, with members taking on stereotypical roles. For instance, if a husband is the abuser, he plays the role of the bully and controller, while the wife plays the role of the worthless one, the wrong one, the partner with no power.

## MAKING CHANGE IN A FAMILY

People involved in one of these scenarios usually say they feel depressed, crazy, or at the end of their rope. Yet, almost invariably they're the healthiest member of the family *because they're the ones who can't stand the craziness anymore.* Relatives who want to continue negative interactions and chaos are less healthy than the ones who recognize that continuing old patterns is the *cause* of the chaos. Craziness is the norm in a dysfunctional family, and health is viewed with alarm. A dysfunctional family uses all of its energy to maintain a sick status quo. When people seeking help understands that their Plan A is impossible—usually some variation of "It's *my* responsibility to make the entire family happy"—they become able to rethink their lives and choose a Plan B that finally allows them peace. When a family is enmeshed in holding on to the problem, instead of striving for a solution, happy family life is an impossibility.

In healthy families, members can sit down together and reassess their Plan A's or formulate a joint Plan B. If you're in a dysfunctional family, however, it may be necessary for you to devise *your own individual plan* if other members refuse to work toward healthy goals. This can be a difficult concept to accept, since it's natural to want to involve others in what should be a joint resolution of your problems.

For instance, if you think it's important to eat family

meals together, yet everyone flies off in different directions at dinnertime, a family discussion on the subject seems natural and logical. But what if, after numerous discussions, you're left at dinner reading the directions on the rice package for company? In healthy families, people listen and respect the needs and concerns of others. If you've stated that sharing dinnertime is very important to you and no one has listened, do you scream, throw things, withdraw, or become irritable? Or do you see that you must seek an *individual* plan since a joint one isn't occurring?

You may say you already have your individual plan—in this instance, you're eating supper all by yourself. But that's the exact opposite of what you really want. With so many outside sports and meetings available, it really is difficult in today's world to coordinate three, four, or five people's activities. You must respect your family members' needs and wishes also. Yet dinnertime is the focal point of shared information and a sense of belongingness that keeps families cohesive. If you find no spirit of compromise or mutual attempt to find a Plan B, you need your own individual plan. Otherwise, you'll stay stuck in feelings of anger, resentment, and frustration.

Your individual plan must be pertinent to *you*. For instance, as a mother, you might announce that from now on, dinner will be served at six-thirty. If it isn't eaten at that time, it's put into the freezer. Or, as a 20-year-old student living at home, you might decide you'd feel more connection living with roommates at school than living with a family that uses home for shower and sleeping facilities only. You might make that decision even if it means taking a part-time job to pay for shared rent.

Your 12-year-old brother has fewer choices. It's true that children have only the power their parents give them. Some kids in our society have too much, but many children in dysfunctional families have too little. The necessity for loving family is built into each of us, and a shared family meal where daily events and conversation take place satisfies a deep need. If your little brother can't make this happen, his individual plan might be to withdraw and seek connectedness outside the family. Sometimes, that connectedness is with friendly neighbors, but often it's with undesirable companions. Young children don't always have the resources for forming good Plan B's.

As the father in this family, you might demand everyone stop their outside activities and come to the dinner table each night. Some fathers can still command this and be obeyed, mostly out of fear. You then have the appearance of a loving household gathered around the dinner table, but they may resent your autocracy and miss the events they love. It's really difficult to choose a good plan when you live among others and they don't wish to cooperate. But when they really won't, you need an individual strategy.

An individual plan must always include your own unique circumstances and be appropriate for the time and place in which you find yourself. And in family settings, individual plans that involve others should be formed only when the old interactions are hurtful and family members refuse to join together and implement a healthier blueprint.

Not all family problems are caused by issues under our control. Though you can choose to get yourself out of debt, leave an unfaithful partner, learn how to respect the ones you love, and stop abusing them, you can't choose not to have illness, death, or unemployment descend upon you. How can you implement Plan B under these unfortunate circumstances? The whole point of Plan B is that it's a choice you make—and, unhappily, you can't choose to make these realities disappear.

*Plan B works whether the ordeals are caused by you and those you love, or are visited upon you by life.* In either case, whether something happens that's ultimately under your control or genuinely outside it, you need to discard a plan that no longer works and choose a Plan B that will enable you to lead a sane, orderly life given your *current* circumstances. In situations that are genuinely caused by outside factors, healthy families can sit down together and find a Plan B that encompasses the new circumstances. Parent-child interaction, fighting at the dinner table, and your partner's neglect are examples of problems you can tackle and change. An infant with a congenital disease, your corporation farming out your division to Mexico, or a drunken driver hitting your car are examples of ordeals outside your ability to control.

## RESOLVING PROBLEMS OUT OF YOUR CONTROL

The story of Leah is a case in point. She entered therapy suffering from depression. She had poor communication with her husband, Roger; her 2-year old daughter, Annie, had cystic fibrosis; and her mother was dying of cancer. She could actively do something about her depression and her marriage, but her child's illness and her mother's imminent death were not under her control. She needed help prioritizing her problems—four at once were just too overwhelming. She chose to deal with her depression and, since it was severe, consulted a psychiatrist for antidepressants. Within two weeks, her depression lifted enough for her to function better, both in and out of therapy. Next, she and her husband learned the principles of communication, and tensions eased a little between them. With these two conditions improved, Leah had the energy to begin to tackle the physical events surrounding her mother's illness. She was not yet able to deal with the emotional impact of her impending death.

Counseling and psychotherapy are a lot like life. Dealing with problems is similar to peeling away the layers of an onion. The outer layers are *there* and easily accessible. They're large and it's easy to see progress as one after another of these layers are removed and the problem becomes smaller. It's also easy to feel successful, because some of the frustrating topics are resolved and dealt with. However, when the inner layers are left, progress becomes more difficult. What remains are most often psychological and emotional issues that are sometimes outside the level of our full awareness.

Such was the case with Leah. She immediately felt better when she moved her mother from a nursing home seventy-five miles away to a hospice that was close to home, where she could visit her mother more frequently. She and her mother were also relieved that the hospice concentrated on quality of life, which included pain medication on demand, rather than the nursing home philosophy of limited pain control, with suffering between each allowable dose.

Leah felt less guilty about the physical circumstances of her mother's illness but still found it difficult to think about her imminent death. That was the remaining core of the onion that made it so hard to say goodbye and help their remaining time be one of healing and completeness. We worked together on what made it so difficult, and Leah discovered long-buried anger and resentment about her mother's perceived abandonment when Leah was eight years old. Her mother had been ill and was hospitalized for two months, leaving Leah with her grandmother. No one had given Leah a sufficient explanation, thinking to shield her from worry. Instead, the opposite was true—Leah fantasized that her mother had abandoned her. Her next thought was one children too often make—that the reason for this was that she was a bad girl and essentially unlovable.

This anger and guilt ran like a subterranean river throughout Leah's childhood, adolescence, and adulthood, causing her depression and clouding every good time and event in her life. The cloud was enough to cause her pain but still enabled her to function. However, when so many problems, both acute and chronic, engulfed her, the depression ate up her energy and resources so that she no longer had sufficient strength to cope with them.

*If you ever have a major family event that involves illness, separation, or other difficulties, always give your child a truthful explanation, appropriate for his or her age.* Children are smart and need to fill in the gaps. If you don't tell them what's happening, they'll make something up, and since children feel they're at the center of their universe, their story to themselves is most likely going to be that *they* caused the illness, the divorce, and so on. If only they had made the bed that night or if only they hadn't argued about homework, Daddy wouldn't have gotten mad and left Mommy. The worst part of this is that this idea goes underground, so that a 35-year-old man or woman may still be carrying around a 5-year-old child's idea, without even realizing it.

Discovering the cause of her depression and dealing with those causes for many months lifted Leah's spirits and energy level, yet she still had the most difficult of her problems to deal with—and the most chronic. Her daughter's cystic fibrosis was heartbreaking to both Leah and Roger. Giving birth to a child with a congenital defect is an example of Plan A being destroyed through no one's fault, and making the very concept of family need rethinking. Anyone wanting children has a Plan A that includes healthy offspring, not unhealthy ones. It's so difficult to give up the long-cherished dream of a healthy child that a great deal of grief and confusion inevitably results.

Yet without eventually relinquishing that dream and forming a Plan B to enable them to live with the reality of Annie's illness, Roger and Leah had no chance for a satisfying future. To do this, Leah came in with Roger to work together on a realistic plan that would take in all the consequences that cystic fibrosis had on their family, both individually and as a family unit.

As long as Leah and Roger clung to their old—and rightful—dream of a healthy child, they would live a life of disappointment and devastation. Their dreams would always be thwarted and their hopes in despair. It took some time for them to be emotionally open to giving up their dream of Annie living a normal life and to slowly form a Plan B that encompassed all that truly was and would be. That plan, painful though it was, had to include frequent and often frightening bouts of acute illness and the knowledge of a shortened life.

It seems strange to say that accepting those extremely sad facts was a liberating event for both of them, but so it was. It became a turning point in their marriage and enabled them to feel close once again, especially as their new communication skills enabled them to talk openly about Annie's illness. When Plan B includes all of reality, the heartbreaking factors as well as the joyous ones, a new pattern of life can be established. This new pattern permits all family members to live without the roller coaster ride of impossible hopes and constant letdowns. It's too wearying to live a roller coaster ride on a daily basis—it's important to find a new stability, with as few ups and downs as possible.

The Plan B that Leah and Roger finally decided upon included the facts that (1) they probably had a limited time with Annie, (2) that time would include many episodes of acute and chronic illness, and (3) this time was all they realistically had. They couldn't increase its duration any longer than the best of medical care could provide. And they couldn't make it illness-free, try as they might. So they decided *in their hearts* that they would make Annie's time on earth as healthy as modern medicine could provide and use that time to show her all the love, caring, and good times they possibly could.

Knowing something intellectually is much easier than knowing something emotionally. Roger and Leah had long ago decided *intellectually* on a very similar plan, but Plan B can never work until it trickles down into your heart. Your heart will always want to override your head when it comes to implementing life's plans. It was only when they could *emotionally* accept the fact that Annie was a very sick child with a limited future that they could arrange a plan that helped them fill their days with love and joy.

Though they neither caused Annie's devastating illness nor with all their best efforts were able to wipe it out of existence, the principles and process of choosing a Plan B were the same as if they were deciding on a new place to live. They needed to form a new dream because the old one had become a nightmare.

Getting off the roller coaster of a Plan A designed for normality, and accepting the Plan B of limited health and a limited future, enabled Leah and Roger to live a sane life again. Remember when in Chapter One we discussed the fact that living with the reality of a situation might be sad, but you won't have to feel crazy anymore? Leah and Roger had been out of synch with themselves—and therefore, their marriage—as long as they fantasized a normal future for their sick daughter. As soon as Plan B included the true facts of Annie's illness, sad as they were, Roger and Leah were liberated from living a life of crushed hopes and broken dreams.

Walking along a level path is always easier than climbing up a steep mountain and then sliding back down again. Yet that's what you're doing when you have a family problem you allow to remain unresolved. I often tell people I could go to China for twenty years and when I returned, still see them fighting, arguing, and feeling crazed by the same old issues as when I'd left. Finding *solutions* for family problems allows each member to live a loving, sane, orderly life. But it often requires major adjustments to individual and family patterns, and some family members may choose not to make those changes.

Seeking a Plan B that gets you unstuck works for all family problems—both the ones visited upon you and the ones you visit upon yourselves. It's the level path that preserves your stamina for the other adventures of life that await you, instead of using all your energy to alternately climb and descend the mountain of family craziness. And, like Sisyphus, you'll be rolling a heavy stone up that mountain, only to see it fall down over and over again. You and yours don't need or deserve to be condemned to that mountain—but only good solutions will get you off.

Finding a Plan B that factors in all your realities enables you to regain your calm, your energy, and your reserves. Then your family can live a new, fulfilling dream, rather than the old one that no longer exists. And if they choose to keep climbing that mountain and rolling that stone, your own individual plan will help you leave that unending struggle and go on to a normal life, inviting the others to join you when they're able. Though it may take months or even years, it's an invitation I see accepted over and over again. And, in the meantime, your family sees and learns as they watch you choose calm, peace, and harmony and move toward becoming your Authentic Self.

# Solutions for Work:
## How to Prevail in the Jungle

Chapter Eight addresses the vast changes occurring in the workplace and what those changes mean for living the Solution-Oriented Life. Perhaps in no other sector do you need to be so alert to the importance of discarding Plan A when Plan B becomes necessary to ensure survival. In no other area is a good method needed in order not to be spun off into chaos. When you are dealing with the self, relationships, or family, a good Plan B may enable you to survive *happily*, but in work situations, you may need Plan B for you and your family to financially survive *at all*, or without slipping far down the socioeconomic scale.

The elimination of blue-collar and middle-management jobs, downsizing, cheap foreign labor, closing and moving corporate divisions, the end of paternalism and loyalty in the workplace, forced early retirement, and the struggle of women to balance career and family responsibilities are issues that people everywhere face in today's world. It's not

difficult in these circumstances to realize there *is* a problem.
It's much harder to think in terms of a *solution* to that problem and then arrive at the right solution for *you*.

In addition, whole industries employing vast numbers of
people are in a state of flux. The health care industry, for
instance, changes constantly, with consumers and providers
alike dissatisfied with costs, payments, and benefits. Hospitals close, nurses are laid off, and managed-care payments
are reduced to a level where doctors and others are leaving
the field. It's hard to feel sorry for physicians, with their
high level of income, but the same scenario is being played
out in other arenas, where a decent salary is reduced by
external pressures to a level that pushes employees down
and out of the middle class.

There's no way to see ahead and guess which career path
will flourish and which will fail. Most of us grew up with
a Plan A that included a long-term, stable job or career
with two or three employers, changing jobs only when and
if a better opportunity came along. And they used to come
along fairly often. That plan no longer exists. Now, it's
most often the employer that initiates termination, and
quite frequently that termination has nothing to do with
the quality of the employee's work.

Another usual Plan A scenario is the dream of owning
your own business. People with this dream are prepared to
work long and hard in an effort to make that business a
success. But with mega-corporations swallowing up competition, and being so cost-efficient they undercut even the
most well-run small enterprise, that dream has also become
difficult to fulfill. How many mom-and-pop stores do you

hear of that have been put out of business by a Wal-Mart or a McDonald's moving into town?

*In today's business world, it's actually dangerous to live with a plan that's even a few years old.* It can lull you into complacency and then you may be blindsided by events that sweep you under. Once you're hit by unemployment and resulting financial difficulty, it may take months and even years to recover. And some people never again reach the level of achievement and socioeconomic status they once took for granted.

## WHERE ARE YOU ON THE JOB?

How can you know when to discard even your most current and up-to-date Plan A and find a Plan B to help you successfully survive throughout your entire professional life? Take the following quiz and see where you stand in today's current labor market:

_____ 1. Are you happy in your present job?

_____ 2. Do you and your co-workers get along?

_____ 3. Are there opportunities for growth within your current company?

_____ 4. Has your industry changed rapidly in the past few years?

_____ 5. Is your industry as a whole a growing one?

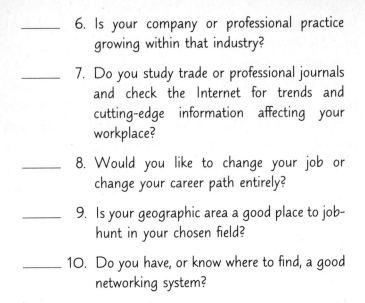

_____ 6. Is your company or professional practice growing within that industry?

_____ 7. Do you study trade or professional journals and check the Internet for trends and cutting-edge information affecting your workplace?

_____ 8. Would you like to change your job or change your career path entirely?

_____ 9. Is your geographic area a good place to job-hunt in your chosen field?

_____ 10. Do you have, or know where to find, a good networking system?

This quiz is different from others in the previous chapters. There really *are* no right or wrong answers to this quiz to answer the way business works today. For instance, it may be wonderful that you love your job, but what if that job consists of making hair curlers or typewriters? Or, you may have answered yes to the fact that your company is growing in an expanding industry but find you dislike what you do and would love to change careers anyway. In no other area is there such difficulty in choosing the right path and satisfying both your emotional and financial needs over a long period of time. The workplace today is truly a jungle, where the weak and unsuspecting are picked off and swallowed up.

How then, can you survive, and not only survive, but *prevail* in this jungle? To do so, you need a *system* that will steer you correctly, not only through the next five years—if that were even possible—but one that will help you respond to changes and shift quickly and flexibly as business patterns alter.

In other areas of your life, it's important to find and implement a Plan B that would be correct for you over a reasonable period of time. Your Plan B might need updating but you could be fairly sure those updates would keep you moving toward the same goal. In today's business world, however, technology and corporate systems are changing at a dizzying pace and will probably do so for decades to come. Industries as a whole evaporate or are globalized, with someone in Malaysia taking over from someone in Milwaukee. Or the very basis they operate from may change drastically.

Whether you work for yourself or for a giant corporation, old workplace tenets and values have shifted irretrievably. Loyalty between employer and employee no longer exists over years and decades, and people who devote themselves to a particular business culture are apt to feel betrayed and bitter when they're downsized or dismissed a few years before their gold watch and pension is due. (The gold watch has probably already disappeared.) Different attitudes are essential, while maintaining hard work and integrity, in order to survive and prosper in today's marketplace.

## A New Attitude

What can this new attitude be? I've defined it as, *"I am my own corporation."* Whether or not you actually incorporate—

more and more freelancers and consultants do so—you need to plan your strategy and career moves the same way corporations do. Just as they have quarterly reports, develop short- and long-range goals, and acquire and divest themselves of companies that will aid or no longer aid them in reaching their goals, so you must learn to do these things and for the very same reasons. If a corporation is successful, it will survive. If not, it won't—it's as simple as that. We all remember Pan Am and Eastern Airlines. They were powerful giants who didn't survive the fierce competition in their field and now they're gone.

The very basis of loyalty has changed in today's market. Though profits were always important, high emphasis was also placed on written or unwritten contracts that recognized loyalty between employer and employee. Now loyalty is almost solely between the corporation and its shareholders, and the bottom line becomes the highest profits possible at the expense of almost all else. Though you may not agree with this cutthroat standard, you need to adjust to this fact if you don't want to be swallowed up, chewed up, and spit out. It's not a very nice work world out there anymore.

How can you live in a cutthroat world, survive financially and emotionally, and maintain your values, all at the same time? If you are your own corporation and examine your status on a quarterly basis—or more frequently, if necessary—you'll be able to spot trends and see events before they come roaring down the track at you. You'll become and remain *proactive*. You'll be able to act, rather than *react*, to circumstances and be much more in control of your work life. The truth of the matter is, if you decide that your Plan B is, "I am my own corporation," you may actually get to keep much of your Plan A.

To see how profoundly life in all its phases has changed, look back to the 1950s. Most women were housewives, and it was rare for them to work outside the home. One income, usually the husband's, was sufficient to support the family. Divorce was extremely uncommon—only Hollywood movie stars got divorced, so families stayed together as an economic unit. Life was generally more settled and sleepy than in today's world.

Forty-five years is the average person's professional life. The 1950s were forty-five years ago. If you were starting out today, think how much the workplace will change in the *next* forty-five years. I remember, at the beginning of my husband's business life, how thrilled we were about his first job and the salary he was offered. We said we'd be delighted if he could stay at that income level for the rest of his career. Well, that total salary would pay three or four months' average mortgage today, without a penny left over for the other eight or nine months or for as much as a candy bar besides. What would have happened if we'd signed a contract for our Plan A?

Once your solution is to become your own corporation, you can think in new terms while maintaining your honesty, work ethic, and integrity. A very beneficial method is to decide that your work life will consist of "joint ventures," just as many corporations form. This way, you can ally yourself with a business or company, work with them on a task for as long as it's mutually beneficial, and part when that task is completed. Though you may not have realized this, *this is how businesses are looking at their relationship with you today.*

If you view your work with an employer in this manner, by being alert to your task nearing completion, *you* can take the initiative to leave the company. You'll become aware you need a new task within the company or realize you must look elsewhere. You eliminate feelings of betrayal you'd have if you thought the employer owed you steady employment based on your competence, industriousness, and loyalty. You'd realize what the management already knows—you're working together for the short term, and who knows what tomorrow will bring.

By focusing on the particulars of your industry, you can adjust your plan accordingly. I mentioned my "quarterly stock-taking" thesis to the general manager of a medium-sized business in the computer field. He burst out laughing and said he'd be left in the dust if he waited for each quarter to keep abreast of the latest changes in his industry. Though your business or corporation may not be as volatile as his, make sure you keep a check on everything happening around you in your professional life. A good corporation does so and steers a steady course between caution and risk.

If you're self-employed or own your own business, Plan B remains the same. You're more likely to actually be incorporated, but incorporated or not, the principles are identical. The system of quarterly reports and finding the next task become even more essential. Wells Fargo evolved from covered wagons delivering mail across the plains to seizing an opportunity to provide banking services in the

West. If they thought their task was to continue delivering the mail as the U.S. Post Office evolved, they'd have been blotted out of existence. Yet they emerged as one of the largest banks in California, and did so when they realized their task had to be transmuted. Another example of understanding the concept of tasks is realizing that a company that considered themselves in the gaslight business would be defunct, but a similar one that realized they were in the light and energy industry might be the giant utility you pay your bills to today.

Monitoring and taking control of your entire working career is the key to long-term solutions for your emotional and financial stability and peace of mind. Whether you're cautious or a risk-taker, you need some security and stability to plan for the future. It's scary in today's world to sign a thirty-year mortgage or plan for children's education, let alone retirement, when you fear your place of employment may disappear and you won't find another job. That's why having Plan B is so essential as you look toward your professional horizon.

There are many Plan B's that help individuals and families find security and relief in planning their financial future. Although your son or daughter may want to go to Harvard, Yale, or Stanford, many states have savings plans where a modest yearly sum ensures entrance to the state university. If the student attends another school, the money is returned to you, sometimes with interest. This is one of the best insurance policies available and one that relieves worry, stress, and tension on the part of parents and children alike.

Another Plan B many people choose as their solution to the long-term work dilemma is to possess so thorough a knowledge or skill that if plants or businesses close they can easily find other jobs. The skill resides not in the geographic location, but inside the employee's head. This is another valuable insurance policy and leads to an important insight. Plan B is your *insurance policy* that no matter what events come your way, you have solutions that enable you to live a good, satisfying, and secure life—and those solutions will allow you to survive life's storms and surprises.

Your overall Plan B must be "I am my own corporation," but there should be subsidiary Plan B's as well. Investing for college or possessing a useful skill are examples of subsidiary solutions, and you can come up with many more for your own particular work problems. Though it's natural to want to hang on to Plan A, the worst thing you can do is hang on for too long and be left in the dust. As soon as you foresee a change, begin to think about a solution. It's OK and understandable to stick with your old dream for a while, but don't make the mistake of waiting so long that there are no solutions left.

## A Downsizing Dilemma

Phoebe learned the hard way how to become her own corporation. When I first saw her in therapy, she was embittered, guilty, and depressed. She had majored in nursing at a prestigious midwestern university and received her R.N. in the mid-1980s. Hospitals were crying for registered nurses with bachelor's degrees, and she was offered an excellent job at a high salary as floor nurse and then, in rapid succession, became charge nurse and head nurse at a large Michigan hospital. She found the work exciting, she was good at it, and her supervisors said she had outstanding skills, both technically and in working with staff and patients.

Five years later, hospitals were undergoing profound changes throughout the United States. Hospital mergers were common and nursing staff was routinely cut in the process. Managed care was also making a big impact, and most hospitals cut costs by ridding themselves of high-priced personnel and replacing them with less costly ones such as nurse's aides and technicians. Many of the first to be downsized were highly trained registered nurses, and Phoebe was one of them.

Four years later, Phoebe found herself working in the East at her fourth hospital. Each time, despite outstanding evaluations, she'd lost her job when managed care practices made hospitals cut staff and substitute L.P.N.'s or aides for registered nurses. After the fourth and last downsizing, Phoebe retreated to her parents' home in a state of depression and, though she was in her mid-30s, was still living there when she came to see me for therapy six months later. She could see no other way but her Plan A, which was to work at the career she had chosen, had trained many years for, excelled at, and loved.

She felt paralyzed because over and over again her Plan A was shot down. She couldn't conceive of a Plan B. She'd retreated to her parents' home to live as a child again and be taken care of, since her adult decisions, though logical, hadn't worked out. She'd lost confidence in her decision making, and though she knew her abilities were outstanding, felt they were useless.

Her depression needed lifting first, since depressed people often feel paralyzed and find it difficult to undertake any action at all. This was true of Phoebe and she was barely functioning. For a short time, she was on antidepressants prescribed by her doctor, and after her mood lifted slightly, she was ready to look at her life and options, though timidly at first. She spoke of her bitterness at hospital management, insurance companies, and life in general. She had been a "good girl" and done all the right things and had been punished anyway. Therapy helped her to see that her "good girl" attitude of trying to please had actually been part of her problem. When she was a child, her parents had been very disapproving of any small acts of rebelliousness but had rewarded Phoebe generously whenever she pleased them, even if pleasing them was detrimental to Phoebe's own gifts and inclinations.

For instance, Phoebe had always loved tap dancing, but her mother forbade tap dance lessons because they made too much noise and she felt they weren't in the same cultural league as ballet lessons. So Phoebe dutifully studied ballet for three or four years, though she never really liked the practice or the dancing. Her mother rewarded her for studying ballet by the unspoken conditional approval she always gave—"I'll love you if you do what I want and I'll withdraw my love if you don't."

Phoebe was smart and she learned the lesson well. She

worked hard, got good grades, acquired excellent jobs, and was well-thought of by everyone. But pleasing authority figures no longer worked in the new impersonal workplace, and she was dismissed no matter how hard she tried. What had worked for Phoebe all her life was no longer working, and she had no rules to live her life by anymore. Using outdated childhood rules had landed Phoebe in neurosis.

Neurosis is trying to make something work in the present that has its basis in the past. It uses reality as a foundation and twines its strands like a vine around the actuality it encounters. The problem is that because neurosis is mixed up with reality, it's difficult to untangle what's reasonable and necessary from our own repetitive banging away at what can't change.

The reality of Phoebe's work situation was that she was very talented at nursing and loved her vocation. Her skills came naturally to her, though she had studied harder in school than necessary, in order to please her parents and professors and make sure she was "the best." Her nursing performance would have been superior without the extras Phoebe gave, some of them because she truly wanted to and others to be seen as the "good girl" again.

Because neurosis is repetitive and operates stereotypically despite changing circumstances, Phoebe wasn't able to see the handwriting on the wall and take proactive steps when she saw aides and technicians invading the nursing field. *She* was being a good girl and doing a good job, so she thought she'd be rewarded as she'd been in the past. It was the only mode of operation she knew. In therapy, she learned that we all yearn for unconditional love; many of us settle for the conditional kind, and some don't even get as much as that.

Phoebe had to learn that her talents and aspirations were on target—that was the reality—but the neurotic aspect of her yearning to be a "good girl" had crippled her. She tried over and over again to take on more work than she should. She thought that could counter trends that were beyond her ability to control—namely, the vast changes overtaking hospitals and the nursing profession.

As Phoebe gained insight into how her parents had squelched her genuine desires and talents and the disapproval they gave whenever she tried to diverge from the path they'd chosen for her, she began to make connections as to how this affected her adult behavior. She saw that she was trying to impress supervisors long after she'd established an excellent reputation, but her supervisors—the current authority figures in her life—were powerless to prevent the downsizing that was ordered from above. Once Phoebe understood this in her heart and not just intellectually, she was ready to untangle her neurotic behavior from the reality of where she found herself. She was ready to find a Plan B.

Phoebe took stock of her position and was sure she should remain a nurse. She was also sure she couldn't stand being laid off one more time. After doing some research, networking within the nursing profession, and speaking to the doctors and hospital managers she knew, she decided to become a nurse-midwife. This entailed a return to school, which she could finance through a combination of student loans, savings, and help from her family.

Phoebe chose this field because it enabled her to become her own corporation—the essential Plan B of the new workplace. The downsizing of the nursing profession was hitting physicians also. Many hospitals were creating birthing suites and staffing them with nurse-midwives, with obstetricians on call if complications appeared. Insurance companies liked this arrangement for the same reasons they liked technicians instead of nurses—nurse-midwives cost less than obstetricians. It was a growing field and her research showed it would continue to be so far into the future.

In addition, it seemed good for mothers and babies. Midwifery is common throughout most cultures and because it is natural, Phoebe liked the fact that it makes childbirth less medicalized. Also, her salary would be much higher performing this specialty, and with more and more hospitals employing nurse-midwives, Phoebe would become able to make her own employment choices, rather than impersonal insurance companies making negative choices for her.

Today, Phoebe is completing her studies. She has long since stopped her antidepressant medication—in fact, she felt gleeful as she threw away the last prescription bottle. Her guilt disappeared when she realized she hadn't been a "bad girl" when she lost her jobs. Being downsized was the result of a steamroller that flattened everything in its path, but she'd found a new sense of self that would allow her to jump out of the way in the future, long before she'd be hit again.

One of the best results of therapy was getting rid of her

bitterness. Bitterness is a venom that poisons the one who is bitter and no one else. It consumes the bitter person and destroys any chance of happiness. It is "stuckness" at its very worst. Once Phoebe was able to discern that her bitterness resulted from the belief that she had no ability to control her life, and that other, "bad" people were doing the controlling, she was able to examine that belief and throw it away.

I believe that approximately 70 percent of how we live is under our control, and the other 30 percent is not. Earthquakes aren't under our control, but we can choose not to live in California. Illness isn't under our control, yet we can live a healthy lifestyle and lessen our chances of falling prey to it. So it's possible to influence even a great deal of events that seem beyond our ability to control. When Phoebe pondered this, she came to the conclusion that her Plan B was to be alert, spot changes and trends in her profession, and explore alternatives so that she could continue to practice as a nurse for the rest of her professional life. That way she would increase her chances of living within the 70 percent of life under her control.

## AFTERMATH OF A LAYOFF

Another Plan B success was that of Morgan. He wanted to prevail in the work jungle, but was failing miserably. He felt like one of those gazelles on the *National Geographic* shows that was about to be picked off by the lion. After years of high pay and respect as a middle manager in a large insurance corporation, he was let go in an effort by the company to remain competitive by cutting staff. In his mid-50s, he tried for eight months to find similar work and finally took a job that involved physical labor rather than remain unemployed. He came to see me with his wife, Jeanne, with complaints of depression, anxiety, and marital problems.

Jeanne was supportive and loved Morgan very much, but couldn't stand the way he was focusing his frustration and anger on her. She had given him an ultimatum—"Get help or I'm leaving." At first, I saw Morgan alone; after he was able to come to grips with the reality of his situation, I began to see them as a couple. Morgan had realized the improbability of finding another middle-management job in insurance, but felt it was that or nothing, because insurance was all he knew. He felt he couldn't continue much longer with the exhausting physical labor, since he probably *wouldn't* be a middle manager again, and he felt like a total failure, old and ready for the scrap heap. As soon as he found hope and discovered the concept of Plan B, and especially the mantra, "I am my own corporation," his depression lifted and he was able to explore different possibilities.

He discussed some ideas with Jeanne, and that's when I began seeing them together. Their personalities and interests complemented each other and they formed a synergetic team. They decided to explore franchising possibilities, since Jeanne was willing to give up her job as a bookkeeper and become the back-office person to his more front-office persona. The more they explored working together, the more excited they became and Morgan's depression and anxiety disappeared. I saw him become enthusiastic for the first time in a long while. Not only did their arguments cease, but they began to actually have fun again together as their planning continued.

Notice how over and over again, as people begin to find solutions for their problems, psychological and emotional disorders vanish and interpersonal relationships improve. This is because staying mired in problems—being stuck in them—produces ill temper, anger, and all those other banes of a happy life. The Solution-Oriented Life eliminates the need for these ailments, which all of us would like to banish forever, and brings enthusiasm back into our lives.

Morgan and Jeanne investigated many franchises thoroughly, and after four months, during which they lived on Jeanne's salary and their savings, chose to open a floor tile franchise. They invested an amount they could afford that was required by the franchisers, who then helped them choose a central location and gave them all the help necessary to get started, including concentrated training in a field that was totally new to both of them. The franchisers were also there to help as the new business evolved—one of the facts that had attracted Morgan and Jeanne to the franchise concept in the first place.

After the store had been open for a few months, I found myself driving by and stopped in to congratulate them. I could hardly find a moment to speak with them because they were so busy with customers. After a while, we had a few minutes to chat and it was evident that their Plan B had given them both a new lease on life. Morgan said he would have done this years ago if he had thought of it—he loved being his own boss and making such a good living. Jeanne said their marriage was better than ever and though she was doing a lot of the detail work, she found she enjoyed working with customers as much as Morgan did. She too said that she wished they had done this years ago.

I've never met anyone who was happy about being laid off, though there is relief from leaving a negative work environment. But over and over again, I've discovered that in many instances, if not most, a good Plan B leads to people finding a better job than the one they left. Morgan found he'd prevailed in the jungle—he was not picked off as he'd feared, but ended up in the fertile grasslands of a business he loved and shared with his wife.

Make a vow today to become your own corporation. Review your present work life. Doing so will help you to thrive and survive where you are, or to cast about for alternatives before negative alternatives find you. The race may not always go to the swift or the strong, but it definitely goes to the aware and proactive. Become that person now and enjoy the *adventure* of change, not the consequences of it.

# SOLUTIONS FOR DEPRESSION:
## Signals for Change

The pain of depression cries out for solutions, but legions of people suffer without relief. Almost everyone is depressed at some time in their life, and if it's happened to you, you know how painful and paralyzing it can be. It's possible to suffer from what psychiatrists call endogenous depression—depression that comes from within. One cause is SAD (seasonal affective disorder), which is due to lack of sunlight in winter months. Other causes may be some cases of postpartum depression; chemical imbalance; or biochemical causes that aren't under a person's control. In my experience, though, most people's depression is of the exogenous type—depression that has an understandable cause, such as loss of a loved one, illness, unemployment, or unresolved painful experiences left over from the past. In these cases, finding and treating the *cause* of depression lifts the misery and despair the patient experiences. Sometimes causes that will eventually become understandable are initially hidden, and the person I see at an initial consultation is completely unaware of the reason for his or her depression.

At times it's possible during the initial interview to determine whether psychiatric evaluation or possible medication is needed. Sometimes this can be determined only after weeks of therapy. But in the vast majority of cases I see, dealing with the cause of the depression leads to changes that eliminates the depression itself.

Depression is so painful that it seems absurd to say it may be one of the best things that could ever happen to you. But if you look back at a time when you were depressed, you will undoubtedly see that depression causes so much agony that you have to change *something* in your life in order to stop the suffering. The problem is that many of us take months and even years to make that change. If you're aware of the source of your depression and learn to recognize its signals when they first attack, you can use them to realize something's amiss in your life. Then you'll be able to short-circuit your anguish and tackle what's wrong. In other words, your depressed mood should signal that your Plan A has gone awry and needs fixing fast, or it needs replacing with Plan B as soon as possible.

But what if you can't find a cause? What if life is going well, yet you find no joy or pleasure in it? If your mood doesn't dissipate within a reasonable time, and you can't for the life of you figure out what's wrong, it's time to seek professional guidance. With help, it may not take long for you to understand the source of your depression. And, as you've seen, understanding the problem is the first step toward finding the Solution-Oriented Life.

Just like anger, *depression is a signal that something is wrong*. As such, it should be welcomed, just as we recognize physical pain as a sign to see a doctor. Anger never occurs unless you feel victimized, so the cure for anger is to recognize its first appearance, and use it to stop and question what's making you feel powerless. Once you figure it out, you can take steps to stop playing that negative role.

The same is true for depression. It is a signal to you that something is amiss in your life, whether something from your past or something from your present. Once you discover what that something is, you can use your newfound skills to see whether your Plan A is salvageable and, if not, what you need to choose as your Plan B. *In most cases, with a good Plan B in place, there will be no more need for your depression.*

Blue moods happen to everyone and may be due to the ebb and flow of hormones, stray thoughts, or the incidents of daily life. But once that mood lasts two weeks or longer, stop and review everything that could remotely be causing your pain. Usually, that's not too difficult. You'll recognize that a breakup with one you love, a serious argument with a family member, or moving to a strange place with no friends or relatives nearby has depressed you. What you also need to know is that *resolving the situation can eliminate the need for the depression itself*. Whether or not you understand the cause of your depression, you may need help in arriving at a good Plan B, and support in motivating you to put it in place. Try doing it first on your own. Then, if you find you're still hesitant or fearful in changing old patterns, I encourage you to see a therapist to help you get unstuck and leave your depression behind.

Oftentimes, endogenous depression—the kind that comes from within—is diagnosed because the person has suffered from low and sorrowful moods throughout life, through good times and bad. But what I've often seen in these situations is that the depression results from childhood events such as abuse, alcoholism in the family, or harsh treatment that systematically erodes self-esteem. The patient often suppresses or does not recognize the pervasive and lingering effect these circumstances have on his or her current adult life and so doesn't have a clue as to why life has no savor.

## ARE YOU DEPRESSED?

Do you react to life's blows by sinking into a depressive state, rather than recognizing depression as a signal to change what's hurting you? The following checklist is taken from *DSM-IV*, the *Diagnostic and Statistical Manual* used by psychiatrists, psychologists, and clinical social workers to diagnose the most common form of depression, called dysthymic disorder. Dysthymic disorder is diagnosed if you've been depressed more times than not for the last two years and have two or more of the following symptoms:

1. Poor appetite or overeating
2. Insomnia or hypersomnia (sleeping too much)

3. Low energy or fatigue
4. Low self-esteem
5. Poor communication or difficulty making decisions
6. Feelings of hopelessness

Major depression is more dangerous and can occur only once, be recurrent, or be combined with manic episodes. In addition to the listed symptoms, major depression may involve markedly diminished interest or pleasure in almost all activities, tearfulness, irritability, significant weight loss, feelings of worthlessness, inappropriate guilt, recurrent thoughts of death, thinking about suicide, a suicide plan, or even an actual attempt.

While it's extremely important to seek immediate help for major depression, too many people let the garden-variety kind—called dysthymic disorder—cast a pall over their lives for years. It may last so long that it feels as if being depressed is a part of you—a part of your very nature. *That's not so*, and the proof I see over and over again is when someone sees life without depression for the very first time. It's interesting that although you may have lived with emotional or psychological problems for 99.9 percent of your life, the instant they're lifted you'll recognize that the "real you" is the healthy, joyful person, not the sick, defeated one. To me this means that we're *meant* to be healthy and full of vitality. That's our natural state—it's our "default" position that we revert to when we resolve our problems and find the Plan B that allows us to live a non-depressed life.

There are other ways to deal with a depressed state. Exercise is very helpful in releasing endorphins from our brains that naturally lift mood levels. St. John's Wort and other herbs sometimes help mildly depressed people and keep them operating on a steady level.

But what if you've tried all this and your depression doesn't yield to a lifting of mood? What if you can't think of resolutions and new plans—in fact, what if you don't have the energy or hopefulness to be able to visualize a way out of your present situation at all? At this stage, psycho-therapy is often helpful, and most times it is all you'll need to get over the obstacle of your stuckness. But in 10 to 15 percent of the cases I see, something more is needed, and that something is antidepressant medication.

## MEDICATION FOR DEPRESSION

Some psychiatrists feel that antidepressants are all that's necessary to relieve depression, and once you've found the right one, they can work. With the pressure of managed-care programs—which have cut mental health benefits drastically and added many more patients to doctors' case-loads—drug therapy is a quick solution to the problem. But if you don't use the time gained from the relief that med-ication affords to find the *cause* of your problem, what hap-pens when you stop the medication? If you don't resolve your problems, either you need to take drug therapy for-ever or you'll slide right back into depression once you've stopped. An exception to this may be postpartum depres-sion, where a small number of women become depressed following childbirth. In this instance, hormonal changes may trigger depression, and medication alone may help. In other cases, psychotherapy may be a useful adjunct, to help the new mother adjust to the vast changes a new baby brings to her life.

Many doctors speak of a chemical imbalance that causes depression, and I agree with them. But which comes first, the chicken or the egg? Though I am not a psychiatrist or medical doctor, my experience as a psychotherapist has led me to an alternate explanation for chemical imbalance. If you become angry and someone checks your blood, he or she will find adrenaline. But did the adrenaline *cause* the anger, or did the anger cause the adrenaline to appear? It's evident that your anger mobilized your body to produce adrenaline to prepare you for fight or flight.

In the same manner, it seems reasonable to assume that loss, abandonment, rejection, entrapment, and all the other causes of depression mobilize the brain to release some chemicals and suppress others. This alters the body chemistry to a depressive state that may sometimes become chronic. Some depressions are so entrenched that antidepressants become the only means to jump-start the body back into more normal biochemistry and give the patient energy to deal with difficult problems. Then the combination of medication and psychotherapy can have a profound impact on a patient's progress, and hope, planning, and a normal mood level can re-emerge.

Medication and/or therapy can be extremely effective Plan B's. Sometimes, antidepressants alone are the keys to a new lease on life. This often occurs in aging people, who are faced with many losses (and anticipate more) and deteriorating health with no hope for improvement. In these instances, antidepressants—which are often combined with anti-anxiety agents—give elderly people a new lease on life. Their moods are lifted to a normal level and they're more able to take part in activities that keep them involved in their community.

There's really no Plan B for the aged infirm that will help them avoid dying. Friends and relations will die, and their own bodies will fail them. Antidepressants are useful here because they enable aged people to utilize their emotional and spiritual resources again and to appreciate the beauty of life, love, and nature. It also helps them to come to peaceful terms with the grand scheme of the universe and their role in it. For the rest of us, if we do need an antidepressant to lift us out of severe or long-lasting depression, we need to use that grace period to work on letting go of the failed script we're hanging onto—our fantasy that will never be realized.

Depression, misery, and despair are often curable if the unworkable patterns of your life are changed. There's a positive correlation between depression and a failed script, and when you learn how to correct your script, the very *cause* of depression can be removed and, therefore, the depression itself will disappear. You won't be depressed if you're living your Unsullied Dream. You may be sorrowful, if external events impinge on Plan A, but as long as your plan is in place and working, depression won't be a part of your life.

If you're living a Modified Dream, you may feel twinges

of depression when items that need fixing are neglected. The Modified Dream is that variation where the first hint of depression is most useful as a sign that an important event in life needs attention now, while it's still minor. It's harder to do this in the Broken Dream stage, where events and depression may have deepened, but it's still possible and worth a try. But if you're in Meltdown, it's likely you're depressed right now and have been for some time.

Loss and trauma are huge issues in the matter of depression. Loss of love, of a job, of self-esteem, of protection, and of finances and traumas such as rejection, abandonment, rape, incest, and becoming a crime victim are also triggers for a depressive state. You may feel depression only once or twice in your life, as the result of a significant negative event, or you may respond with depression to incidents that wouldn't inspire that response in others. My experience is that when the latter is true, it may be that you suffered trauma as a child. That trauma may then resonate throughout your life and make you respond more deeply to negative circumstances than you would if your childhood had been safe, happy, and secure. Try to look back at your early years and see whether you can discover an event that stimulates depression in your present life when you encounter a similar loss or fear.

## DEPRESSION FROM THE PAST

Simon and his wife, Neela, were having marital problems, and Neela had insisted they go for counseling. She com-

plained about the lack of love in their lives recently and
Simon's lack of interest in "fixing" this. It became clear
during the interview that Simon was depressed and that
perhaps when that was dealt with, the problems themselves
might disappear. In other words, the depression might be
*causing* the marital problems. This isn't an unusual situation, and it's easy to see why. Depressed people have little
energy to devote to their lives, and what energy they do
have is often expressed in irritability and anger. Depressed
people are also negative, so they don't see hopeful solutions
to problems. All this was true for Simon, which is why he
and Neela agreed they should put marriage counseling on
hold while he came for individual therapy.

At first there was a question as to whether Simon needed
antidepressants in addition to psychotherapy. He was so
slowed down by his depression that it was doubtful he
could function enough in his life and in therapy sessions
without it. But after three or four meetings, his depression
lifted enough for him to decide to forgo medication. I often
see this initial lifting of depression after a few sessions.
Only a little progress has been made in terms of discovering causes, but what's changed dramatically is that the
patient now has hope. In almost all situations, *genuine
hope—which is a good Plan B*—can be offered.

At first, Simon had to borrow my hope for him. He felt
so depressed, that he couldn't believe he would ever feel
differently—a common feeling among depressed people.
But he trusted me and, after a few sessions, began to hope
on his own. He could see where he wanted to go, but
couldn't yet see how to get there. The therapist's job is to

be a guide out of the thicket of depression—out of the Plan A of an outworn fantasy. As Simon began to explore his life, he could see more clearly what his fantasy was that he was holding onto so tenaciously.

He'd been brought up in a small, conservative town in the South where everyone knew everyone else. His father had divorced his mother when he was two, remarried, and moved two states away. Except for three or four visits in his childhood, he never saw his father again. Though other men in the town befriended him and tried to act as surrogate fathers, Simon had been abandoned by his father at a very vulnerable age and had felt deeply rejected ever since. As he got older, he noticed he was the only boy without a father to attend soccer and Little League games, and felt more and more like an outsider.

Childhood depression hasn't been recognized very well until recently, and boys especially are able to cover it over with aggressive behavior. Simon became a bully—he unconsciously figured that it's better to hurt someone than be hurt. In other words, his Plan A was, "If someone needs to get hurt in every relationship, I'd rather be the *hurter* than the *hurtee*. It's better to be like my father than like myself and end up hurting so much inside."

As he grew to adulthood, he gradually gave up active bullying and became more subtly domineering in his work and personal life. This characteristic appealed to Neela, since her own upbringing had made her a passive young woman who was dependent on authority figures. A great number of marriages are made when two neuroses mesh, as they did with Simon and Neela—but they're rarely mar-

riages made in heaven. The very characteristic we unconsciously long for is the one that ends up driving us crazy.

When Neela began to chafe under Simon's domination,
she became resentful and didn't act as loving as she once
did. Then Simon tried to demand her love, which made
her angrier, so she withheld her love still more. This vi-
cious cycle is what triggered Simon's depression, but there
were other marital problems that encouraged it as well.
Underneath Simon's dominating and independent manner,
he still felt like an abandoned 2-year-old. Any 2-year-old
is very dependent, and an abandoned one still more so. As
Neela retreated more and more, Simon's dependency deepened and increased his depressive state.

Before Simon and Neela's marital problems could be
successfully dealt with, Simon had to understand the reasons for his negative behavior and its consequences. Otherwise, there'd be no hope for a solution and long-term
happiness in the future. Simon was eager to find these
causes and we began to work together as a detective team,
looking for clues that would explain his pain and hurt.

At first, the therapist is the lead detective. His or her
training and experience help the patient explore the likely
paths and hidden lanes to find the clues that will make
sense of behavior that's seemingly nonsensical. Simon began to speak of his childhood years, remembering the pain
and sorrow of his father's abandonment. He began to
weave the strands of his childhood story with the strands
of his marital story; as he recounted more and more incidents and feelings, he began to see a hidden pattern. He
stated that it was something like a Polaroid photo—at first

it's blank but soon a picture begins to emerge, and after awhile the portrait becomes crystal clear.

Now Simon became the lead detective and I took a back seat. More and more events and emotions became available to him, and he became eager to make the connections between his childhood loss and his adult problems. He recognized how he'd felt that none of those surrogate fathers could ever take the place of his real father—as indeed they couldn't—so he rejected all help from anyone. His bullying and dominance were methods to take whatever he could get and cover up his dependency needs. But whatever he could get was never the love he really sought from his father and would never have.

Simon's depression cleared when he became aware of his previously unknown motivation. He realized that by seeking a love that was impossible to attain, he was forgoing all the love available to him in his present life. He wanted a Plan B that allowed for love and understood that the dominating behavior of his old Plan A would eventually cast a pall on everyone around him. For the first time in his life, Simon was able to want a more balanced relationship.

At this point, I saw Simon and Neela together for a few sessions. Neela was happier, but now her own dependency needs weren't being met. She both wanted equality on the one hand, and longed for dependency on the other. This contradiction explains why neurotic people are rarely happy. Whichever need is being satisfied leaves the other need unmet. That's why so many relationships go round and round in an unending, unsatisfactory manner.

Now it was Neela's turn for some individual sessions.

While she wasn't depressed, her own dependence would no longer be satisfied as Simon lost his need to dominate. The balance of their marriage was upset—even though it hadn't been in happy equilibrium for a long time. Neela agreed that she wanted more of a true partnership but didn't see how she could change.

She began to explore her own reasons for being the way she was and told about her own parents' marriage. Neela's role model for a wife's behavior was her own mother. Her mother had been subservient to her father, who would turn red in the face and bellow whenever anyone opposed his wishes. The one time her mother had rebelled by starting her own tailoring business, she'd failed, and Neela's father hadn't let her hear the end of it for a long time. So Neela learned not only that passivity and dependency are a woman's lot, but that it's dangerous to rebel against a man—the authority figure in her life. Her failed script, hidden from her conscious view, was written like this: "I can only survive as a woman if I keep quiet and acquiesce to what the man in my life decides is good for me—*whether or not that's what I really want.*"

Neela was shocked that she was living her life by a code she consciously rejected. The more she became aware of her hidden Plan A, the more she decided that if it wasn't in Meltdown yet, she'd like to hurry it along. She followed the same process Simon did—the adult Neela searched for the clues to the origin of her own unhelpful needs. Once she found them, she examined whether she wanted to be like her mother and emphatically decided she did not. When she examined decisions initially made by her childhood mind, she realized she'd outgrown them and, for the first time, wanted to choose appropriate ones for her adult life. She was no longer the slave of unconscious, hidden needs. Her needs became adult instead of childish, and she too wanted a marriage based on true partnership and equality.

At this point, Neela and Simon met together and marriage counseling began in earnest. They both wanted the same Plan B—a happy marriage based on *interdependence* and equality—but didn't know how to get there. Their joint Plan B became, "We want a marriage based on a shared arrangement of ideas, work, and decisions, and we choose to be an equal team." Now that Simon can seek love from Neela without the need for dominance, and Neela can find her needs met in an equal relationship, Simon has no need for his depression any longer. He's able to receive love now because his adult self has decided to give up longing for his father's acceptance and instead get the love Neela's happy to give. He's thrown away his failed script that in order to avoid vulnerablity and hurt, he needs to be dominant and aggressive in all his relationships. His depression is gone because Plan B has given him hope and a blueprint for a happy, meaningful future.

Depression is a habit that people fall into when they don't know how to overcome their problems. Learning how to live the Solution-Oriented Life means learning a new *habit* that will help you eliminate 90 percent of the garden-variety depression that afflicts people today. Habits by their very nature are repetitive and semiconscious at best. Therefore, to form a new and better habit, you must be very conscious of your new pattern for a while.

Depression and the Solution-Oriented Life are inversely proportional. The more depression you have, the fewer solutions you'll find, and the more Plan B's you find, the less depression you'll have. Nowhere else is it so plain to see that forming a *habit* of seeking solutions leads to positive emotions, and a zest for life is impossible without it. Failed scripts lead nowhere but down. Make up your mind not to live that way anymore. You deserve to live in the light, and your chances of being depressed are lessened the more your blueprint for life is realistic and not an outmoded fantasy.

An outmoded fantasy is a failed script—it's just not working anymore, if it ever did work in the first place. Living with failure is a recipe for bad feelings and low self-esteem. If you try and try to make something work that *can't* work, you'll fail at life over and over again. What happened to Terry is a case in point.

## BREAKING THE DEPRESSION HABIT

Terry recognized a pattern in her life and she was sick of it. Craig was the fifth, and Terry hoped last, in a long string of boyfriends who were hypercritical, put her down at every turn, and in general made her feel bad about herself and her life. When she was with these men she felt depressed rather than good, but she felt even worse when she broke up with them and was alone. She'd generally stay in these abusive relationships for a year or two and then end them, only to find someone who looked different from the last guy, yet acted exactly the same. Now she'd been with Craig for a year and a half—she was right on schedule. She'd broken up with him three weeks before scheduling an appointment, which she did for two reasons. The first was that since the breakup she felt more depressed than ever; the second was that for the life of her she couldn't figure out why she chose such ill treatment. As far as she could see, all she wanted was to be loved and cherished. So she came to therapy to overcome her depression and break her longstanding involvement with emotionally abusive men.

Terry had the insight to realize her choices weren't accidental but rather the result of some pattern she couldn't understand, and so she began to look at her whole life history. She soon discovered that criticism and harsh judgment had entered the picture very early on. Her mother had been an unhappy woman, thwarted in her efforts to become a professional singer. Instead of rewriting her script and finding a Plan B that allowed her to sing in the church choir or in amateur groups, she lived with her outmoded fantasy—a failed Plan A—and took her bitterness out on Terry, an only child. Irritability is a sign of depression, and Terry came to the conclusion that her mother had actually been depressed for as long as Terry could remember.

Terry tried to gain her mother's love and sought to please her. But since her mother's depression had nothing to do with Terry, her efforts failed; she endured her mother's critical, biting behavior as long as she lived at home. Her father worked long, hard hours, traveled a lot, and, in retrospect, Terry felt, stayed away in order to avoid his wife. So Terry had no ally to help her and provide another role model as she grew up.

It seems obvious that Terry should seek as boyfriends, kind, loving men who would provide her with the care and affection she lacked early in life and craves so much. So why does she punish herself by finding exactly the opposite of what she wants—someone just like her mother? This scenario is so common that often observers feel that people like Terry are masochists—purposefully pursuing abusive partners to punish themselves for imagined crimes. Though sometimes there's some component of this type of thinking, nothing is usually further from the truth.

Instead, Terry and so many others like her are seeking *mastery* over the early events in their lives. This thinking is largely unconscious, but goes something like this: "If I can find someone with the same traits as my mother (or who-ever caused the original damage) and get *them* to love and cherish me, the original knot that caused my problems will become unraveled and my life can finally go forward smoothly from now on." Terry's unconscious Plan A dream was—restated in Plan A terminology—"I want to be happy and loved, and the way to achieve this goal is to find a person who will put me down and lower my self-esteem, the way my mother did—but I'll get him to love me." Ob-viously, this is a disastrous formula.

The problem with this blueprint is that in order for the magical thinking to work, the person chosen must have the same traits as the original figure—and *someone with those traits, by definition, cannot furnish the love and affection that will provide the cure.* Not only that, the pain and hurt that comes with being on the receiving end of verbal and emotional abuse, sarcasm, and put-downs is compounded by the original feelings of rejection experienced as a child. In other words, there's a synergetic effect, and it hurts more than twice as much—it hurts beyond belief. So when Terry broke up with Craig, the natural upset of the breakup was made much worse by the old feeling dwelling within Terry of being rejected by her mother.

Terry was 28 years old when she decided to change her life's pattern. But the part of her that sought and chose Craig and all the other emotionally abusive men in her life was a hurt 5- or 6-year-old who lived unexamined within herself. When a child constructs a reason for the way her world is made, she must of necessity do so from a child's point of view. It's 6-year-old thinking that forms the idea of finding someone like Terry's mother to undo the original damage. A 28-year-old examining that statement would instantly dismiss it as something that could never work—and what's more, would see the impossibility of choosing another impaired person and expecting that person to act in a mature, loving manner. Terry needed to discover the bankrupt Plan A she was living by, and she worked hard to do so.

Psychotherapy works to relieve depression and other ailments by assisting people to recover hidden Plan A's they're living by—Plan A's formed by a little child and never re-examined because they're hidden from conscious view. What therapy did for Terry, and what it does for so many people, is help the old habitual thinking rise to the

surface of her mind and be explored by the adult person
Terry has become. In this new, open arena, anything examined that's good can be kept, and anything that's harmful can be rejected. For instance, Terry had been brought
up to be honest and trustworthy. She liked those traits and
wanted to retain them. But she saw the bankruptcy of her
*relationship* patterns, and the adult Terry utterly rejected
the idea that someone she chose now to undo past hurts
could undo the pain and depression caused by her upbringing.

Terry began to understand the origins of her own depression and why she was attracted to emotionally abusive
men. She understood that their abuse only reinforced the
old depression she felt from her mother's rejection when
she was a child. She was able to become 28 emotionally as
well as chronologically, and the adult Terry felt she could
now get what she wanted. Her Plan B became to seek love
and caring from a healthy man who'd be able to provide
these things. She was willing to look in appropriate places
and wait for someone suitable, no matter how long it took.
She wholeheartedly felt that this tactic was much better
than involvement with someone who would cause her pain.
Though it's been a year and she hasn't met a suitable partner yet, she recently called to tell me that though she's
alone, she's not lonely and hasn't felt depressed since she
formulated her new plan.

If you see unhealthy patterns in your own life and suffer
from depression, try to see whether the people you choose
for friendships or love relationships resemble parents or
others that caused you pain in early life. If you find a strong

resemblance, you can be fairly sure you're living with an unconscious Plan A you created as a child that has no hope of leading you to successful relationships. If you can figure this out on your own and make the necessary connections and changes, do so. You'll then be able to form a Plan B that has no more need for old, unhealthy patterns. From that time on, you can achieve positive relationships with friends and lovers—and a solution for your depression.

But what if you're married or involved with someone you chose precisely because he or she was verbally or emotionally abusive or in some other way resembled an old, hurtful pattern? The only remedy in the end *may* be a breakup of the relationship—yet I've seen many people change in a healthy direction once the injured party refuses to suffer anymore. When the victim decides not to be victimized anymore *and no longer needs the victimization—that old, unconscious Plan A*—the familiar pattern no longer works and the abuser either needs to leave or to change. And in an impressive number of cases, he or she does decide to stay, and so the old, unhealthy pattern finally alters for the better.

So many people say, "Not *my* husband," "Not *my* wife," or "You don't know *my* mother—she'll never change!" But if you don't *need* to have someone in your life who'll abuse you, you'll *want* to choose a Plan B. Your spouse, parent, friend, or colleague will test and retest you to see whether you mean business, but once they discover you do, they will have no other recourse but to change if they want to remain in your life. That's why counseling and therapy are so often successful when the "perpetrator" never even enters the office.

Terry felt depressed when she was involved with abusive men. When she left therapy, she needed to use any feelings of depression as a *signal* that she'd met another abusive guy and run away as fast as she could. If these depressed feelings didn't appear after at least six months in a new relationship, she could be fairly sure she was living her Plan B. Notice that I said *after at least six months*; that's because abusive relationships don't usually start out as abusive, but begin with all the positive aspects of healthy ones. It's only when the victim is "hooked" that, slowly but surely, the abusive pattern begins.

When people feel trapped, they can lash out. But if they feel they can't, they often submit and become depressed. If you feel depressed, look and see whether there's any person or situation that makes you feel this way. If so, see whether there's a connection between that problem and your depression.

Using a good Plan B to find solutions gets rid of the *need* for depression. If you're feeling trapped, look for Plan B and don't let fear stop you. Follow the Plan B system. Reread the early chapters and realize that you won't and don't need to change until you're ready to do so. Live with your plan and let the pros and cons drift in and out of your consciousness. It takes time to be ready for new possibilities. Entertain the notion and live with the potential for change for as long as it takes.

A fantasy that can tell you much about your current depression is to envision magically being rid of your problem.

If it's a love relationship, you're out of it; if it's a work one, you've quit; and if it's a family one, you just moved across the country. Then see how you feel fantasizing living with that situation day after day. If you realize that your depression would leave you, you know you need to fix your Modified or Broken Dream or find a new plan entirely.

Getting rid of the cause of your depression is one of the major ways of getting unstuck from your problems. I urge you to do so and become like so many people I see who rediscover joy and enthusiasm when the burden of their depression is lifted. Many of them describe it in one of two ways—either as a black cloud that's lifted from their shoulders or a great weight that's been lifted from them. In either case, it's clear they felt their problems were weighing them down. Life carries a heavy enough load as it is—don't add to it by carrying depression on your shoulders. Lay down your burden, let it go, and walk with anticipation through the door of your future.

# SOLUTIONS FOR ANXIETY:
## Taking Appropriate Action

Anxiety, simply put, is caused by disquieting thoughts that go round and round in our minds—thoughts known as worry. Chapter Ten will teach you how to reduce or eliminate this enormous drain of energy and end the circular thinking that prevents you from finding solutions. As the Bible states in Matthew 6:27, "Can any of you by worrying add a single hour to your span of life?"

Anxiety is a signal we must respect and pay attention to—just as we must pay attention to the signals of anger, depression, frustration, and other negative emotions. *Anxiety means something is wrong with our feelings of safety and security, and we should heed that warning.*

You may say that when you're worrying, you have no problem paying attention—in fact, anxiety occurs when you pay too much attention to your problem. But it's probably not the right *kind* of attention. When you're anxious, you perceive a danger, but you short-circuit any solutions for it by thinking in a circular rather than linear manner. For instance, if you worry that no one likes you, it's easy to get on the treadmill of thinking, "No one likes me," and then enumerating all the examples you can find that will reinforce that idea. Next time you return to that thought, your anxiety will be greater than before, but what will have occurred to make you more popular? Nothing at all.

What if, instead, you learn to think in a linear manner? Instead of going round and round on the treadmill of fear and getting nowhere, what if you learned to apply the Plan B concept and *went forward* toward your goal with a solution that would dissolve your anxiety? If you could choose a Plan B that would make you popular, would you be anxious any more? Probably not.

## How Anxious Are You?

Before we go any further, let's see how the *DSM-IV* diagnoses anxiety, so you have a clearer picture of what it is and can tell whether you suffer from it.

Anxiety disorder must consist of excessive anxiety or worry more days than not for at least six months about a number of events or activities. It must be difficult to control the worry, and you must experience at least three of the following six symptoms, also more days than not, for at least six months. Here are those symptoms:

1. Restlessness or feeling keyed up or on edge
2. Being easily fatigued

3. Difficulty concentrating or feeling your mind going blank
4. Irritability
5. Muscle tension
6. Sleep disturbance

If you see by this checklist that you suffer from anxiety disorder, there are many things you can do to get better. Though medication is probably the last route to take, it's comforting to know that anti-anxiety medication can be very effective in reducing symptoms and enable you to feel normal again. In addition, certain antidepressants contain anti-anxiety ingredients, and some antidepressants are recognized as being very effective in also reducing obsessive-compulsive behavior.

Obsessive-compulsive thoughts and actions cause worry and torment to those who suffer from them. Obsession consists of thoughts that come to you unbidden and just won't leave you alone. Compulsion is the necessity to commit acts in spite of yourself, such as excessive hand washing or stepping over sidewalk cracks. Obsessions and compulsions usually respond well to medication and behavioral techniques. But I've seen people who suffer from these symptoms become much more relaxed and bring their symptoms well under control when they deal with (usually) undiscovered problems that caused the original anxiety. Obsessive-compulsive behavior is designed to cover up that anxiety by drowning your mind with so much white noise in the form of worrying, or so much distraction in the form of repeated, compulsive tasks, that there's no room to pay attention to the anxiety that's causing your problems. By discovering the cause of the anxiety and then implementing a Plan B that dissolves it, the very need for obsessive thoughts, worries, and compulsive acts diminishes or disappears. There's nothing to cover up—and no need any longer for distractions or white noise.

*The most effective remedy for relieving anxiety on a permanent basis is to pay attention to that first twinge, take time to discover what your worry's about, and then take appropriate action to relieve the cause.* Plan B, by definition, will be the appropriate solution, but before you can ever find a Plan B that's right for you, you need to recognize that anxiety is the white noise that prevents you from thinking clearly.

Many people suffer distress primarily because they can't eliminate enough of that noise to assess their situation realistically. It's difficult to face modifying Plan A and impossible to think of implementing Plan B when you're paralyzed by fear. Fear is caused by anxiety about the future, and no change is possible until the reasons for that anxiety are explored. Remember, you are in control of taking the first step for change, and you do not need to take it until you're ready. But you need to clear away a space in your head where exploration and clear thinking becomes possible. Here are four good techniques for doing so:

## 1. Jot It Down
The easiest and most common technique, requires only a small notebook or notepad that you carry with you. Whenever something occurs that seems worrisome, jot it down immediately so it will be out of your mind and onto the

paper. Then it'll be available to you later when you have more time to pay attention to the matter. This method works because if something seems important enough to worry about, you may need to keep it going around in your head just to remember to deal with it at a later time.

This is also a useful method when you find that worrying is keeping you from sleep. Turn on the light, write down your worry, and have it out of your mind and down in your notebook to deal with in the morning. Jotting it down is such a commonsense technique that most people use it in some form or other. The problem is that either they don't use it all the time, or their anxiety is so strong that this method can't contain all their worry. If this is the case with you, the following methods may be more suitable and help you worry less.

## 2. The Stop Sign
Close your eyes and picture a stop sign. Visualize it very realistically—its redness, the octagonal shape, the white letters saying Stop. Now, every time you find yourself anxious or worried, stop, close your eyes for a minute or so, and imagine the stop sign. Repeat this every time you find yourself worrying, and within a week or two you'll be worrying much less.

The third technique is not unlike the stop sign approach and works for much the same reason.

## 3. The Calm Scene
Close your eyes and picture a pleasant scene from your life, past or present. It could be a sandy beach you love, a farm

scene or a peaceful lakeside view. Fill in the scene with birds flying, soft breezes, clouds drifting overhead, the smells surrounding it, the animals that would be there. *Make it real.* Fill it with as many sensory details as possible. Keep your eyes closed for a few minutes and get the scene fixed firmly in your mind. Do this every day for a week and then decide whether this is going to be your calm scene or whether you'd like to change it for another one.

After the first week, any time you feel anxious or find yourself worrying, stop and immediately go to your calm scene. Spend a minute or two immersing yourself in it. You'll find when you're finished that you won't be quite as anxious. Go on with whatever you were doing, and if you catch yourself becoming anxious again, *go again to your calm scene*. Repeat this as often as necessary.

Two things will probably happen. You'll find over a period of a week or two that you're spending less and less time feeling anxious. So you'll spend less time in your calm scene during each episode and fewer times going back to it because you're not allowing yourself to indulge in worry, but are short-circuiting it each time. In other words, you're not reinforcing the bad habit of worry but are instead reinforcing a new habit of calm. The other reason is that the stop sign or the calm scene itself become the *symbol* of calm to you and so visiting them immediately helps put you into a state of relaxation.

## 4. The Worry Hour

This technique seems both odd and humorous, but in practice will demonstrate beyond a shadow of a doubt how wasteful is the time you spend worrying. It works like this: Choose an hour every day that you'll reserve exclusively for worrying and a special place where you'll do it. Let's say you choose between seven and eight P.M. every evening and you'll worry in your favorite armchair. Whenever you begin to worry at any other time, write down the item worried about; then go to your worry corner at seven P.M. During this hour you must do the exact opposite of what you do the other twenty-three hours—*you must worry* and not allow your mind to wander from that task. Two things should happen. The first is that you'll consistently interrupt your worry cycle during the rest of the day, the second is that you should find it difficult to seriously worry for a solid hour.

You'll probably find, over a short period of time, that you'll decrease your hour of worry to a half-hour and even less. You'll also become accustomed to clearing your mind from worrying during the rest of the day, which will leave you more able to concentrate on *the solution to worry— taking appropriate action.*


You may say that all four of these techniques are tricks and you don't want to play tricks on yourself. Yes, they are tricks, but tricks are useful for breaking a debilitating habit—the worry habit—and they *work.*

These techniques, however, are only the first useful step to lessen the fear and dread that prevents you from assessing your life in the Plan A/Plan B format. They decrease the white noise that's drowning out your ability to think clearly and preventing you from the linear thinking you need to take you toward your goal. You'll use these methods to clear a space where *you're* in charge—not the terrible worry habit.

High levels of anxiety often correlate with the number of changes you need to make in your life, or when current events recall old, anxiety-producing issues of safety and security. In either case, the small-step approach is useful. Don't be afraid to explore causes and options, *remember, you don't have to change the smallest detail of your life unless and until you're ready to do so.* Once you're sure of that, exploring options can become an interesting and useful fantasy, instead of something frightening you *ought* to do.

"Oughts" and "shoulds" cause many problems in people's lives, but if you allow yourself space for a Plan B to develop, those two words can disappear from your vocabulary, and instead a calm "must" can take its place. A good Plan B becomes a "must" because it's the logical and realistic plan that fits who you really are and what you really want in life. And that "must" won't be fraught with tension and dread—instead there'll be a calm recognition that you're becoming the person you're meant to be, instead of the worried, tense person you've become.

Many times, your "oughts" and "shoulds" come from old, forgotten precepts you decided you needed when you were very young—your old, unrecognized Plan A. Then, even though they're no longer true—and perhaps never were in the first place—you feel anxious when you break these rules. Until you figure out what your Plan A is, and decide whether it's still necessary in your life, you can be at the mercy of anxiety whenever you make an adult decision that violates the old code.

## AN EXAMPLE OF HIGH ANXIETY

Patrick, a young man in his late 20s, sought psychotherapy because, as he put it, he was "bouncing off walls." He was used to living with a very high level of anxiety, which he'd come to think of as normal, but he recognized that this time was different. It all started when his company transferred him from Chicago to New York. He was in the financial department of a large development company that had its headquarters in the New York area and he'd been offered a big move up the corporate ladder. He'd received a large raise and a generous bonus, and had found a nice apartment in Manhattan. He should have felt happy and secure.

Instead, ever since he'd moved to New York six months earlier, his anxiety had reached proportions even he couldn't tolerate. When I first saw him, his speech was so pressured that I had a hard time understanding him. In his anxiety, his thoughts flew from one worry to another and it was hard to slow him down enough to help make sense of his problems.

Gradually, what was worrying him became clear, though Patrick still had no explanation for the *why* of it all. It seemed that in Chicago, he'd made friends he felt comfortable with. They often went out after work in a large group that he enjoyed, though he was never close to anyone in particular. When questioned about this, he said emphatically, "I never want a best friend, or to marry or live with anyone." He insisted that this was the way he was, he was happy with it, and he didn't want to pursue the issue.

Patrick calmed down slightly because he finally had a place to unload his worries and concerns. Though his tension level was still very high, he was able to focus on *what* worried him. He realized that whenever he was with others, whether on or off the job, his anxiety heightened because he felt the need to please them—and not just to please them in general, *but to please them by being perfect*. And naturally, since he was merely human, he fell from his pinnacle quite often and became devastated and frightened.

Many people have a need for perfection, which really comes from a deep sense of inadequacy. If you're feeling unconfident and insecure, then you may try to gain feelings of competency by striving for perfection. Striving for perfection is different from striving to be the best you can be. You can see this in athletes—they strive to do their best, but when they fail, as they sometimes do, they take it in stride and try again the next time around. But people who must be perfect have no tolerance for the least mistake, and are crushed and berate themselves whenever their humanity interferes with their impossible fantasy—their faulty Plan A. *And they're usually totally unaware of what that Plan A is.*

Patrick became aware that he had this syndrome, once he accepted that fact, he became eager to explore its origin. More than anything, he wanted to be rid of the burden his anxiety caused that filled him so full of fear. He looked for the root of this unhelpful trait and realized that he'd been like this for as long as he could remember. After many sessions, he recalled that his younger brother had been labeled "the bad one." As so many people do, he then decided at the age of 3, 4, or 5, to formulate a Plan A that would "solve" the problem. As a little child, what made sense to him was, "I'll make up for my parents' suffering from my brother's bad behavior by becoming 'the good child' and being perfect."

This made sense to his child's mind and was reinforced by his parents' giving him praise and affection whenever he was quiet, helpful, or pleasing. He saw their frustration and disapproval when his brother misbehaved and fantasized that he'd lose his parents' love altogether if he was "bad." Over the years, he'd become completely unaware of his Plan A and never had an opportunity to examine it and find out whether it really was viable or needed scrapping.

Once Patrick became fully aware that his adult self was operating under childish and false assumptions, he finally became capable of figuring out *why* he was so anxious. Though he was still wary of having close friends and rejected the idea of ever committing himself to anyone because of the risk of displeasing them, he began to see the connection between needing to please his parents and needing to please the current people in his life. He began to talk about his feelings with "the old gang" he hung out with in Chicago. They were people he'd worked with for five years who accepted him, and he knew exactly what would please or displease them—and above all else, while maintaining a facade of closeness, going out in a group prevented real intimacy with any single person. Even so,

Patrick spent an inordinate amount of time being exqui-sitely tuned in to the group's reactions to him, which in itself used up a good deal of his emotional energy.

Finally, he was able to see what made him so terribly anxious when he moved to New York. In any job reloca-tion, it takes at least three months to get used to new rou-tines, new associates, and a new setting. Mistakes are common as new details are learned. In addition, real estate in Manhattan is expensive and hard to find. Patrick worried that his apartment choice was imperfect, so he never invited anyone up to see it. He was surrounded by strange peo-ple—colleagues whose opinions, values, and desires he didn't know. All these things made Patrick feel insecure and left him without the ability to know how to please everyone and be "perfect."

Patrick's lack of perfection under these circumstances threatened to overwhelm him since his unconscious Plan A had no chance of success. He *couldn't* be perfect, make no mistakes, and please people all the time. This is an impor-tant point to remember—if you feel you're breaking down under the stress and worries of life, you can be pretty sure your Plan A is broken and needs looking into.

Patrick's anxiety had become so intolerable that he knew he wanted help to find a Plan B that would allow him to live a calmer emotional life. But first he had to examine his Plan A—and once he did, he decided it needed total dis-mantling. His brother, who now lived in the Midwest, was still a pain in the neck to the family, causing minor prob-lems and disagreements as a matter of course. Patrick didn't have much to do with him and saw him only at infrequent holiday gatherings.

Patrick's adult self saw that he was a separate being from his brother and that, as a child, he really had no power to make up for his brother's actions. In fact, though his parents were appreciative of his cooperation, they would have rejected his plan to be perfect for them. It really upset him to realize that he'd spent most of his life following a bankrupt script he was unaware of, and that friends and colleagues were not expecting him to be the perfect person he tried so hard to be.

It took him a while to get over his anger at himself, but he finally decided to channel that anger in a useful direction—finding a Plan B that would offer a solution to his terrible anxiety. He saw that his perfectionism would have to end, and it was comparatively easy to let go of the part that came from his role of being "the good son." It wasn't so easy to let go of the need to be perfect that came from his sense of inadequacy and failure.

Patrick was eager to solve this problem as he felt some of his anxiety drain away. He wanted to be "normal" and get rid of all of it, and we spent some time discussing his need to become "perfectly normal." By now he was able to laugh at himself, and saw how he was falling into the same trap all over again—wanting to be perfect at being normal. Slowly but surely, he learned to value himself for the attributes he really had: his honesty and integrity, his loyalty, his intelligence and curiosity—and most of all, just being Patrick.

He worked very hard to achieve this goal, and he knew

he'd arrived when he chose his Plan B. It was "to live the life of a human being, with all its complexities and imperfections and not the life of a deity." He sighed with relief when he spoke of giving up the unconscious God-like role of perfection he'd chosen so long ago. With his usual determination, he noticed the reactions of others to mistakes he made at work, and saw that his colleagues reacted to them for what they were—his getting up to speed on the learning curve of a new job. He tried inviting a few people over to his apartment for a pasta dinner and recognized they had a really good time, even though he'd spilled a drop of red wine on the tablecloth.

In short, he began to have realistic expectations for himself and, as he did so, his anxiety and worry became less and less. But every day for almost a year, he had to repeat his Plan B to himself and remind himself that he was choosing to live his life as a human being—his *only* choice, really—and not the impossible one of a perfect god. Patrick understood that he'd been trying to become someone he could never hope to be, and that it had led to his feelings of anxiety and failure. The appropriate action Patrick took to escape this was to examine the rules he was living by, discard them, and choose other, more realistic ones that were compatible with his humanness.

Before he left therapy, Patrick enlarged his Plan B. He realized that part of his anxiety came from loneliness and his inability to share thoughts and feelings with others— they'd see he wasn't perfect. As he feared other people seeing his imperfections less, he realized he was no longer afraid to try having a close friend or two. His Plan B became "to live as a human being in all its aspects, which includes having close companionship with others."

When you live life with a Plan A that doesn't take care of your safety and security needs, not only do you live with anxiety, but you're not living up to your capacity to be *you*—in essence, you're living an inauthentic life. Usually, it's inauthentic because it's constricted in some way, as Patrick's was when his perfectionism interfered with any possible intimacy with others. Any constriction or distortion in the way you were meant to be prevents you from fully blossoming into your Authentic Self.

If you're suffering from any form of anxiety, stop and think about how it's distorting your life. Sometimes, anxiety originates from childhood distortions in thinking, as Patrick's did. Other times it arises from current problems that need addressing but get put off because no solutions seem viable. The case of Heather shows how outworn Plan A's need replacing as soon as possible in order to end intense anxiety and prevent events from escalating out of control.

## ANXIETY AND LIFESTYLE

Heather had suffered for two years from stomach-churning anxiety before she decided she needed professional help. When I first saw her, her nail biting, hair twisting, and other nervous mannerisms detracted from the attractive woman she really was. Just about to join the 40-somethings, her anxiety extended beyond facing middle age as a single, divorced woman. Most of it stemmed from her extravagant lifestyle.

It seemed that for nearly a decade, Heather had been a successful telecommunications salesperson. Her salary plus commissions totaled in the low six figures. It would certainly seem she could afford all of life's extras. So it seemed to Heather too, and she spent money lavishly on whatever she wished. But Heather didn't keep a budget, and because her friends and associates also had high incomes, money flew out the window, spent on vacations, clothes, restaurants, and an expensive condo.

Heather watched her credit card charges build up monthly by hefty amounts. At first, she didn't think too much of it, especially since she had quite a few, so she was unaware of the grand total. But around two years before I met her, Heather asked for a small loan and was denied, saying she had too many charges outstanding. That was the first time Heather added up all the totals and was shocked to find she owed $50,000. Not only did this total almost half her annual income, but she realized she was paying over 15 percent a year in interest, so even without charging one more item, her debt would increase by $7,500 per year.

At this point, Heather's lifestyle was so out of synch with her income that she couldn't even envision ending her credit card charges—all she could think of was to charge less each month. She certainly couldn't see how she could pay off any of the balance. She began to keep track of the accumulated debt, both in new charges and in accruing interest. When she reached $60,000 she began to panic, and she essentially lived with that panic until she came for help.

She decided to buy no new clothing and eliminate vacations, but she couldn't give up eating out with her friends. She tried to pay cash and not use her cards, but often she'd be short and she'd pull out a credit card. Still, she cut her spending by a good deal—it just wasn't good enough. She was unable to pay off enough of her debt monthly to make a large enough dent in the $60,000 (and growing) pile, and the annual bonus that she had hoped to use to pay off a large chunk of debt was used on other shortfalls for her condo expenses.

When we first met, Heather was going round and round with so much worry that we spent the first few sessions on a broad outline of how we would work together to solve her problem, which gave her some hope. We also discussed specific techniques she could use to interrupt her worry habit. The technique Heather liked best was the calm scene—she felt it cleared her head the most and eliminated the constant buzz of anxiety that prevented her from thinking clearly. And she realized she needed to think clearly to take appropriate action.

Heather knew that who she truly was was not the tense, anxious, irritable woman she'd become—but she also knew she wasn't frugal or penny-pinching. It became clear that her Plan A had been "to spend as much as I wish because there'll always be enough" and this plan had evolved because for as long as she'd worked, her income had increased greatly each year. Her unexamined assumption was that this would continue indefinitely and that this year's expenses would be covered by next year's bonus, so that she was always spending more than she had *this* year.

Heather was now able to understand that her anxiety was a signal that something was askew in her life, and she clearly saw what it was. But try as she might to discover a Plan B that would work—not the obvious one of "I'll spend no more money," because she would never implement that plan—she could think of nothing she could live with.

It took a long time for her to deal with her reality, and it happened only after she couldn't meet even her minimum monthly payments. At this point, her anxiety became so acute that she was ready to face whatever it took to make it go away. She was ready to formulate her Plan B and realized that any delay in doing so would only increase her problem. The Plan B she arrived at was scary to her because it meant a fundamental change in lifestyle. It was "to get out of debt entirely and not fall into the debt trap ever again."

She brought in a budget—the first she'd ever done—and as she examined her expenditures, she couldn't find enough expenses she was willing to eliminate. When I suggested more drastic changes, Heather was horrified and refused, but after more sleepless nights and continued physical symptoms, she gradually came to terms with the radical measures her solution required. She was firm in *wanting* her Plan B, but found it difficult to implement the actual plan that would get her out of debt entirely.

Some weeks after this, Heather came in looking more relaxed than I'd seen her in months. She had thought over the choices we had discussed and was relieved. Her "ought" had finally become a calm "must." Now she attacked her budget with bold changes. She announced that she had put up her condo for sale and would move into a small but pleasant rental apartment in a more modest neighborhood. She should clear about $30,000 from the sale, which would pay off half her debt. She'd made an appointment with Consumer Credit Counseling, which is an excellent non-profit group with a toll-free number. It works with consumers and lenders to work out methods of repayment. They demanded she turn over all her credit cards, and it took her two weeks of panic until she decided to do so. They'd come up with a budget and we went over it together.

It was bare bones, but it allowed her adequate money for basic necessities, and that's what she'd have to live on for the next two years. Because her income was so high, she'd be able to pay off her remaining debt of $30,000 plus interest in that period of time. Heather found herself feeling exactly the opposite toward her Plan B from the way she had felt a few months earlier. Now she felt calm, positive, and optimistic, while previously she'd felt nervous, negative, and pessimistic. What had caused the change?

Heather had put off a solution to her problem—Plan B—because no solution seemed viable. As her anxiety became overwhelming, what had seemed impossible came to be seen as not only possible, but imperative. What was true for Heather is true for you also. *The longer you put off solving a problem—often while it's still small—the more your problem can fester and grow, the more difficult your solution will be, and the more anxious you'll become.*

Most people practice denial at times, and for some people it becomes a way of life. Denial eliminates anxiety, since you don't deal with your problem or even think much about it. But the fact that it's still *there* means the consequences of that problem continue to accumulate, and then a day of reckoning comes.

It is much better to face your problems when you feel that first twinge of anxiety, while your problems are still small. Then, a Plan B that's not so drastic may be more than enough to resolve the situation. Taking appropriate action at the beginning may consist of a plan that's much less radical than the extreme measures you'll need later. Heather's cutting back spending by only 10 percent when she first became aware of her anxiety's origin, or an alcoholic attending AA meetings when he's fired from his first job, instead of entering rehab once his wife's divorced him and he's been unemployed for a year, are examples of this proactive behavior.

You won't need to deny the true circumstances of your life now that you have a system to work with. You have the tools to take appropriate action with a good Plan B. Heather's Plan B to "get out of debt entirely" could have been implemented earlier with much smaller changes in lifestyle. The same plan, put into effect when catastrophe loomed, meant her life was turned topsy-turvy. She also would have eliminated two years' worth of severe anxiety that affected her mind and body.

Anxiety increases as life careens out of control. Actions— or the lack of them—create consequences that pile on top of each other until a mountain of change is required to resolve a situation that was originally only a small molehill in your path. If Heather had taken the appropriate action of (1) paying attention to her original signal of anxiety, (2) looking for its likely cause, (3) sifting through the steps necessary to find Plan B, and (4) implementing that plan, she could have saved herself two years of distress and a debt that was leading toward bankruptcy.

Usually we don't look at what's bothering us because we're afraid of what we'll find. The sad truth is that the ostrich who buries his head in the sand most often gets a kick in his butt. What's more, because his head is buried, he can't see where danger is coming from, or run away from it. He's stuck. Getting unstuck requires seeing, hearing, and feeling everything that's happening. If you see, hear, and feel everything that's happening to you, a red flag will pop up when something's wrong. *Anxiety is a red flag of the first order*. Permission to take time to gear yourself up for change and use the small-step approach that prevents you from feeling overwhelmed hastens your ability to find Plan B and prevents extra anxiety from forming.

Taking appropriate action about cares and concerns eliminates the need to go round and round on the worry treadmill, and eliminates fear in the process. The Plan B you finally choose will be the appropriate action necessary to dissolve the tension and stress that have been your recent or lifelong companions. Once anxiety and dread evaporate into thin air, the amount of energy you have available for life can multiply tremendously. Worry and anxiety are not the companions you need—calm and optimism are much better friends.

# SOLUTIONS FOR EXTRAORDINARY CIRCUMSTANCES

Life feels better when it's within our control, whether Plan A is going well or we've shifted to Plan B—choosing our mates, our careers, our surroundings, and the way we spend our leisure time seems the right and natural thing to do. And for most of our lives, we don't question what seems to be that natural order of living—we take it for granted.

But sometimes life throws us a curve. Most of us face some period of time when every avenue seems cut off and no Plan B appears possible. Then we need to face the fact that there *are* no solutions within our old order of thinking, and a previously inconceivable plan must somehow be imagined.

For many people, problems exist that are totally out of their control. Many of the serious issues of life fall into this category: death, divorce, infertility, becoming unemployable, and illnesses such as cancer, Alzheimer's disease, or

AIDS, or being the family caretaker for someone with these illnesses. Then no Plan B seems to make things better—indeed, no Plan B seems possible. Your loved one will still die, your spouse will leave you, you can't have your own biological child, you aren't able to work anymore and need an income, or you or someone you love are the victim of a dread disease.

## No Ordinary Solutions

If you're going through a traumatic event where no ordinary solution seems possible, take this quiz and see whether your problem falls into one of the following categories:

_____  1. Do you or someone you love suffer from a crippling or devastating disease?

_____  2. Do you or someone you love suffer from a terminal illness?

_____  3. Are you the caretaker for a family member with a serious illness?

_____  4. Has someone you loved died in the recent past?

_____  5. Have you become unemployable through illness, disability, or other reasons beyond your control?

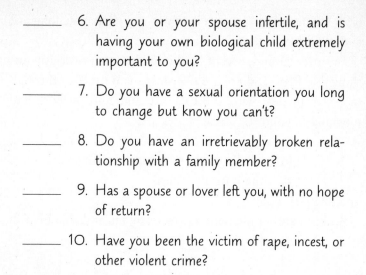

_____ 6. Are you or your spouse infertile, and is having your own biological child extremely important to you?

_____ 7. Do you have a sexual orientation you long to change but know you can't?

_____ 8. Do you have an irretrievably broken relationship with a family member?

_____ 9. Has a spouse or lover left you, with no hope of return?

_____ 10. Have you been the victim of rape, incest, or other violent crime?

If you answered yes to any one of these questions, you suffer from a problem with no ordinary solution. The old order of life has been shattered, and radical new plans are needed. If you answered yes to two or more questions, you're going through a period that *demands* new solutions even though none seem possible. Chapter Eleven will help you assess your present psychological and emotional state, come to terms with your present situation, and devise a solution that will help you pluck peace, purpose, and meaning out of the surrounding chaos. *Even if life is very difficult, if you're living Plan B, you can find peace in the midst of pain and sorrow.*

Plan B is meant to overcome obstacles. But when those obstacles are brick walls that can't be demolished or side-stepped, what then? What if every Plan B you can think of is unsatisfactory, and you'll never get what you long for and can't live without?

In order to find, accept, and implement a previously unthinkable Plan B, there are five stages you must go through in order to deal with the calamity and find purpose and meaning beyond it. These stages are:

1. Take immediate action to limit the damage.
2. Deal with the current issues.
3. Mourn your loss.
4. Find and implement a previously unthinkable Plan B.
5. Live your Plan.

## 1. Take Immediate Action to Limit the Damage

When disaster strikes, you need to mobilize as quickly as possible and take immediate action to limit the damage and escape further consequences. Calamities and disasters have stages, just as other events do, and the first stage in any disaster is the crisis period. This is the stage where access to expert help and advice is so beneficial. Advice from experts assures that you'll take the *most appropriate* action for your circumstance. The best surgeon and hospital, the best treatment, someone who's looking for a new employee when you've just lost your job, the nearest agency that helps people in your situation, are invaluable to limiting damage. As bad as the trauma is, taking immediate action limits damage and prevents further consequences.

Though your action must be fairly immediate, it should not be impulsive. Impulsive action may actually worsen circumstances, so though decisions must be made quickly, never be impulsive—check your plans with friends and experts. And if you find you're too overwhelmed, confused, or frozen to function at your best, choose a trusted friend or relative to take over for you until you're well enough again be in charge.

## 2. Deal with the Current Issues

After you've taken immediate action, the next stage is to deal with the current issues. Plan A is very important when tragedy strikes, because even small changes can make an enormous difference when dealing with serious illness and loss. By using as many of the still-workable aspects of Plan A as you can, you'll be able to stabilize and maintain as much of your former life as possible.

For instance, if you can no longer walk because of a car accident, a motorized wheelchair or handicapped transportation service can alleviate your lack of mobility. Your normal Plan A of getting from one place to another must be modified, but you'll still be able to get where you want to go. Or, if you're taking care of a sick relative and need respite care, finding family or friends or calling a helping agency can get you out of the house and give you room to breathe.

This stage blends with the next, the mourning stage, because to *need* the wheelchair or to *need* to ask for help involves mourning losses of physical ability and independence. But if these are current issues that will impede dealing with the traumatic event, it's important to understand what your present needs are, in order to lessen your burden. By doing all you can to use what's left of Plan A, you'll be able to function as fully as possible.

I see many people who have a great deal of trouble dealing with current issues. Men especially feel it's somehow un-

manly to ask for help, and some elderly people find it difficult to accept assistance, even though for most older people
Medicare will provide home health care free of charge, if
needed. Asking for assistance, even if only on a temporary
basis, arouses feelings of dependency, inadequacy, and loss
of control that prevent many people from helping themselves recover from divorce, illness, or other serious events.
It's especially important to talk over these feelings with
someone you love and respect to avoid falling into the trap
of depression and becoming a permanent host to your traumatic event. It's a given that you can't live with the Plan A of
your Unsullied Dream when disaster strikes. Though a previously unimaginable Plan B is necessary, utilizing as much
of Plan A as possible makes life easier, and provides Plan B
with the underpinnings that allows it to function.

### 3. Mourn Your Loss

Mourning is the process we go through when our lives are
wrenched apart. It drags us down into the depths of despair, but it's a normal, healthy process that helps us let go
of what can never be again. It ultimately helps us rise to a
new life. Whether it's loss of a loved one, loss of our own
or another's health, or loss of our lifestyle, mourning is the
mechanism that releases us to our future. So when you're
faced with traumatic events, allow yourself the time to
mourn, with all its attendant feelings.

You may feel paralyzed or unable to comprehend the
magnitude of changes needed; you may rant at fate; you
may feel you'll never be able to face life again; the future
is closed to you. But eventually—and each person differs—

it's time to pick up the pieces and not only get on with life but get on with it in a meaningful way. It's time to find a solution, when you can't even figure out where or how to begin—or what that solution might be.

## 4. Find and Implement a Previously Unthinkable Plan B

The solution begins with accepting the reality of your loss, and that can happen only after genuine mourning. Whether it's loss of a limb, loss of eyesight or hearing, loss due to death, or loss of independence, no solution is possible until you accept the reality of where you are at the present time. The direction in which to go in order to reach your goal is determined by your present coordinates. The goal is Plan B—a solution to your current ordeal— and you can't begin to reach that destination until you acknowledge your present reality.

Trying to implement Plan B without accepting your current situation is like living in Massachusetts and trying to reach California by going east instead of west because you insist you're really living in Hawaii—you'll never get there. Likewise, you'll never reach your goal of a solution to your problem until you accept the physical and emotional geography of your present landscape.

Accepting your present reality is a kind of neutral ground. You've cast off enough of the past to see your current situation clearly, but you don't necessarily know the direction your future will take. Your present reality is what *is*—it's the link between your past and your future.

This stage is usually a time of feeling empty and depleted. The tumultuous feelings of the mourning stage have lessened, but there's not yet a feeling of any purpose in life beyond getting up, putting one foot in front of the other, coming home, and going to bed. But it's an important stage because nature abhors a vacuum and after a time, the empty space will need to be filled.

### 5. Live Your Plan B

Finding and implementing a sensible Plan B for a radically new situation is the task at hand when no ordinary solutions are viable. It's a Plan B you never dreamed you'd need to entertain, but lo and behold, the impossible has entered your life. And whatever your circumstances, *your new Plan B must find purpose and meaning in life, no matter how limited or transformed that life may be.*

Jim Brady and Christopher Reeve are outstanding examples of people who transformed meaningless tragedy into purposeful crusades that can inspire and change society. In doing so, they transcended their original life's scripts. Most of us can't aspire to their heroism, and we sit in awe at what they've accomplished. Their power and abilities were taken from them, one in a cruel and one in an accidental manner. But they found new power—the power to change aspects of society—because they found a Plan B within themselves that restored their purpose and meaning.

Both of them did what we would all do—they explored and took advantage of every medical and scientific treatment that might improve their lot. They tried to hang on to as much of Plan A as possible. But when all that was accomplished—when no more physical gains were immediately possible—they had to come to terms with the limits their new situations entailed. They needed to search for a radically different Plan B.

Plan B usually arises from the ashes of Plan A. For example, Roy's eyesight was very poor and getting worse. His Plan A was obviously the same as everyone else's—to see objects with decent vision. As his sight worsened, his Plan B was to have an operation, use thicker lenses, use brighter lighting, and so on. But a time came when he had exhausted all his Plan B's and had to face the fact that nothing was working any longer.

Linear thinking was no longer possible. The straight line from a Plan A of seeing decently to a Plan B of seeing as well as possible using new, innovative methods was no longer open to him. His vision was fading and he had to face the Meltdown of all his plans—normal as they might be—and realize he needed a plan for being blind.

This was such an unacceptable idea that his thinking process ground to a halt. This is what often happens when most people face unthinkable, impossible events. But these events only *seem* impossible—they occasionally happen to each and every one of us. And after a period of paralysis and denial, a radical new plan needs to be devised or we won't emotionally survive—and Roy followed these stages as well.

He finally decided to attend classes at Lighthouse for the Blind, which taught him Braille and the many things necessary to navigate his world, literally and figuratively, as a blind person. He's now changed his job and is functioning quite well. He had been a telephone lineman; since he wasn't able to work at that any longer, he asked for and received retraining. He now has a desk position at the telephone company, where he uses a special computer developed for the blind.

Living your Plan B is the result of all the stages Roy, and each of us, must go through in order to continue to live the Solution-Oriented Life when that life seems out of reach forever. *The Solution-Oriented Life is never out of reach.* Purpose and meaning are always available, but they may be hard to find unless you deal with each stage of your trauma thoroughly.

Even when death stares us in the face and shatters all our plans, choosing love, taking care of unfinished business, and saying goodbye is a choice we can make. The condemned man on his way to the execution chamber can express remorse for his crimes and ask for forgiveness. He won't rescind his death penalty by doing so, but he'll have regained some dignity and humanness—a solution that will end his life's story on a more meaningful note. A woman lying on her deathbed with only an hour to live might create more purpose and meaning than her life has had for a long time by telling her family she loves them and showing them peace and acceptance in the face of death. *We always have a choice.*

All the previous chapters have been predicated on the fact that choosing Plan B when Plan A is irretrievably broken works and makes for a good life. In this chapter also, you can choose a productive life that has purpose and meaning. It may not be happy in the traditional sense of the word, but you can find a peace and calm you've never known by living through an event you'd never volunteer for. And a life with purpose and meaning leads you to becoming your Authentic Self.

Purpose and meaning are the solutions as long as we're alive. The Solution-Oriented Life is available and necessary as long as we have breath, and the only real solution is to find purpose and meaning in the new life that's given. The problem is, that in the face of disaster, we reject our new circumstances and all our old solutions are impossible. Think of people dispossessed by earthquakes, tornadoes, or war, losing their homes and everything they own, often in a single moment. Or think of hostages or political prisoners, mistreated and alone, with no knowledge of whether they'll ever be released, or even survive. Finding a new purpose and a new meaning is imperative for emotional survival, and some people hit by catastrophe never achieve it. Then, though their physical bodies survive, their psychological and emotional selves cease to exist. They are empty shells.

The family whose home and possessions were erased by war or an earthquake must leave the area where they may have lived for decades and leave neighbors they've known all their lives. They may feel there is no more purpose to their lives, but after survival issues are settled, they must find a new reason for being, or risk their family's emotional health and cohesiveness. The wonder of being human is that most people do achieve this, and families go on to live productive lives.

The story of the Iranian hostages taken in 1979, is another case in point. Though shackled and blindfolded and forbidden to talk, they survived by surreptitious communication, mental games, and a spirituality they summoned from within. They also dreamed of freedom, and the dream kept them going day after endless day. It's hard to think of surviving in that atmosphere, but their very purpose became to survive until they could be free again.

The family stricken by war and the hostages in Iran had no ordinary Plan B's available. Their immediate Plan B was survival moment by moment. The family whose village was destroyed had their choices limited by military, food, and climatic factors. The hostages in prison had almost all their choices removed except the choice of inner dignity.

Disaster changes us so much that we become different people. Hopefully, it deepens our spirit and makes us wiser and more profound. But it can also traumatize us so much that we don't function as fully and freely as before. If you suffer from a circumstance where there are no solutions to issues of life, health, or economic freedom, you must employ the Plan B of mourning your loss, facing the reality of your circumstances, and finding *your* purpose and meaning within those limitations.

Your own purpose and meaning are essential, because well-meaning family and friends may attempt to help by trying to impose *their* ideas on you. Because we're unique individuals, what has purpose and meaning for someone else may be meaningless or depressing for you. This is a battle you must fight, with allies of your own choosing—a trusted friend, minister, or counselor to help you in the process.

For instance, some of my most rewarding work has been to help dying people find a sense of meaning and peace. It helps them end their life story with a sense of completion and gives me the satisfaction of seeing them content, instead of tormented. Though their physical body is dying, their spiritual and emotional self is being healed. But sometimes relatives want them to keep on with aggressive treatment that will yield very little in return for much suffering. Then I help that person weigh the benefits against the costs and help them decide when enough's enough.

This is a major reason why the hospice movement is achieving such acceptance and growth in this country. People recognize that giving dying people a chance to end their lives in dignity, among family and friends, keeps the meaning of their lives intact.

Even when dreams are broken, your Plan A can still work if you figure out ways to mend the brokenness. But when Plan A has gone as far as it can and there's still no hope for the Plan B of a normal life, the only solution is *acceptance* of the calamity and a transformation of your attitude toward it. *The Plan B of a new attitude is the most helpful tool you'll ever have to find a solution to your overwhelming circumstances.*

Elisabeth Kübler-Ross, author of *On Death and Dying*, became famous for publishing the five stages of coming to terms with death: denial, anger, bargaining, depression, and acceptance. Though death and other afflictions are things we fight against with all our might, there comes a time when acceptance is the only solution to finding peace and purpose again. It's never possible to accept the *rightness* of murder, incest, or the death of a child, and that's not the acceptance I'm speaking of. It's accepting the *reality* of the event—that it did happen, all that could be done has been done, and the future is irrevocably changed. This acceptance of the reality of the event is the first step in the change of *attitude* necessary to discover a Plan B that gives life meaning again.

## FINDING MEANING

I remember Nora, a 42-year-old teacher with two young sons, who came to see me three years after she'd been diagnosed with breast cancer. Her left breast had been removed, but further disfiguring operations were required when the cancer spread. One day, her husband came home, announced he couldn't deal with her illness any longer, and walked out of the house and right out of their lives.

Nora couldn't support herself, her sons, and her costly medical bills on her teacher's salary alone and Dave, her husband, had taken off. By the time I saw her, her parents had promised to help her financially, so her material Plan B was in place. But she was suffering from depression, which originated from suppressed rage and the real possibility of dying and leaving her two sons behind. She'd been so busy living her plan that she felt that giving in to her anger at Dave would destroy her ability to function. Instead, her rage went underground and turned into a pervasive depression. She was so scared of looking at the possibility of death that she had no realistic plans in place for her children.

I helped Nora deal with her depression and assisted her in making good plans for the children in case the worst happened. She became able to face that possibility more easily once she knew her sons would be taken care of. But Nora may have helped me more than I ever aided her, by showing me the determination, courage, and love that a human being is capable of under the most adverse circumstances. The Plan B she formulated was to leave her children to be brought up by her aunt, who agreed to do so. She and her parents agreed they were too old, and her aunt, who was much younger, had the strength and energy required. It's no one's plan to die and leave our children to be raised by others. Knowing that her aunt would raise her sons lovingly if she couldn't be there to do it herself gave Nora calm and peace as she lived day by day.

Finding a totally new purpose and meaning in life is the only solution to a catastrophic problem. It's the only Plan B that will work in a satisfactory fashion. Nora's solution was to live as long as possible to bring up her sons and to know they had a safe haven if she died. Though the solution must be a purpose that works for your own life, it often has a side effect such as the one that Nora had on me—and I'm sure on others. And that side effect, though not purposely thought of or planned, has a meaning that's as important as the one you've crafted for yourself.

*That purpose is to be a role model to others.* All of us struggle with overwhelming problems at one time or another, and most of us are lucky enough to find one or two people we look up to as models for the way we want to live our lives. We admire their pluck and mettle and it gives us courage to do the same. Ordinary people who have gone through a particularly difficult time with grace and bravery are usually unaware of the positive influence they've had on others, and are surprised when told they've been so inspiring.

Of the many people I've been privileged to help who have struggled through terrible times and given me back more than I ever gave to them, none have inspired me as much as Loretta. When I tell her this, she's genuinely surprised and doesn't quite understand how this can be, but it's so. Loretta was sexually abused by her father from the age of six, with her mother's silent knowledge and complicity. Now a good wife and mother to three girls, her parents still emotionally mistreated and terrorized her as an adult and she felt she had no power to stop them. They called her "the bad one," and what's worse, she actually believed it.

As if this weren't enough, she'd been diagnosed with lupus and had suffered with it for the past five years. When I first saw her, not only was she physically ill, but so emotionally sick that she could do nothing but rock back and forth and hardly speak. The precipitating factor was her belief that her father was abusing an 8-year-old cousin who lived next door to him, and Loretta was afraid to report it and bring down more of her parents' wrath upon her head.

I explained that legally, I would have to report this to the authorities, and Loretta admitted that one of the reasons she came to me was that she half-consciously knew this to be so. But since her father was known in the community, the police illegally gave him warning, and he was able to threaten the child to lie, "or else." So not only did nothing come of the accusation, but her cousin most probably continued to suffer sexual abuse.

The effect this injustice had on Loretta was devastating. The only people she trusted were her husband and daughters. When we met, she openly told me she didn't trust me but had nowhere else to turn. When she saw I was outraged and was taking action to stop her father's molestation, she began to trust another human being outside her family circle for the first time. But when I failed to protect her cousin, she lost faith in me and had to start rebuilding that trust all over again. Not only that, but the outcome reinforced Loretta's belief that her parents were all-powerful and could do whatever they wished.

Loretta needed antidepressant medication and it helped stabilize her. But the emotions rekindled by her cousin's plight exacerbated her lupus and she was hospitalized on three separate occasions. As I visited her and visibly cared about her welfare, Loretta finally came to place her trust in me and we were able to form a strong working alliance.

None of Loretta's Plan A could be rescued. Her normal wish to have loving, protective parents and a healthy body were obviously in Meltdown. It took eighteen months for Loretta to deal with all the ways her father's abuse and her mother's ignoring her most basic need for protection had affected her life. Her rage at them and disgust with herself for not being "stronger" were major issues we dealt with in every session. It took a very long time for Loretta to absorb the truth that if she refused to deal with her parents, they had no ability to interact with her any longer. She felt they could arrive on her doorstep, invade her house, and verbally and emotionally abuse her—and the only thing she could do to prevent this was to hide.

Finally, she understood with her heart that as an adult she had the right to say who could enter her property and who could not. The next time her parents appeared and refused to leave, she called the police and told them she had trespassers—a drastic but necessary measure. Her parents stopped visiting but began making abusive phone calls, calling her obscene names. Loretta got an unlisted number.

As Loretta took these steps, which were scary to her, she began for the first time to find the strength and power an adult uses to resist being victimized by others. Her parents' attacks over the years had left her feeling powerless and childlike, and finally being the victor had a profound effect upon her. Gradually, her anger and depression diminished—and as it did, a lovely young woman began to emerge. Timidly at first, and then more and more confidently, Loretta began to explore who she really was. As she did, she gained confidence in her ability to function and make intelligent choices and realized she was a capable and optimistic woman, in spite of all her afflictions. Loretta began to dream of a Plan B that could work despite the extremity of her circumstances.

There were no normal solutions for Loretta's life. Though her parents were still very much alive, she decided she could have nothing to do with them ever again and that they were dead to her. The few times they'd been in touch in the recent past, Loretta spent days recovering from the ordeal. This solution was a great relief to her, and over the next months I watched Loretta blossom into a new person. After she rid herself of the belief that she was dirty for what had been done to her, she discovered she was a very spiritual person. She joined a nearby church and, over a period of time, finally felt worthy enough of love to feel that God could love her. She reported that she had made friends with some members of the congregation, and these were the first friends she'd ever allowed herself.

Loretta's journey followed the five stages necessary for coping with extreme situations: (1) She took immediate action to limit the damage by entering therapy and taking antidepressant medication to pull herself together and continue to function. (2) She dealt with the current issues by trying to intervene to help her cousin and by taking steps to prevent her parents from continuing to abuse her. (3) She spent a long time in therapy mourning the loss of her childhood and of normal parents' love. (4) Finally she was able to accept these sufferings as reality—they had happened and nothing would or could change that fact. She spent surprisingly little time mourning the loss of a healthy body, since, as she described it, the emotional anguish was so terrible that physical pain was nothing in comparison. She was able to find the previously unimaginable Plan B of claiming power over her mind and body as much as she could, and dismissing her parents and her fear of them from her life. (5) Then Loretta lived her Plan B.

There's a sweetness to Loretta that she doesn't understand and that she rejected for a long while, but it's this sweetness and her optimistic nature that draws people to her. I often asked how she could handle the physical manifestations of her lupus, which are considerable, and she answered that life was so good now that just to open her eyes in the morning, see the sunrise, and have people she knows are her friends makes her glad to be alive.

Loretta humbles me. I'm in awe of her ability to triumph over all the adversity in her life. Every day she struggles with an illness that's been unfairly visited upon her. But Loretta has found a solution. She found her Plan B when

there *was* no solution. And though Loretta is mostly unaware of it, she shines as a role model every bit as inspiring
as the most famous politician or movie star could ever be.

Loretta has found purpose and meaning in life, in spite
of terrible hardships. Most of us, thankfully, don't have to
overcome as much adversity as she did. Yet what does purpose and meaning consist of? What are the common
threads without which life loses its savor and becomes mere
existence? The next chapter will help you find the Ultimate
Solution—the Plan B that allows you to live your life with
serenity and peace, no matter how difficult the situation.

# THE ULTIMATE SOLUTION:
## Living the Good Life

Life is a paradox. We spend much of it pursuing the things we feel will bring us happiness, yet when we attain these goals we often feel bored, restless, and discontent. Even with the optimum career, spouse, and socioeconomic status in life, most of us don't relax with our gains and coast happily through the rest of our lives. We usually want more, even if we don't know what "more" consists of.

It helps to realize that life consists of stages, and our needs differ as we reach these different levels. Ecclesiastes puts it so well:

A time to be born, and a time to die;
A time to plant, and a time to pluck up what is planted;
A time to kill, and a time to heal;
A time to break down, and a time to build up;
A time to weep, and a time to laugh;
A time to mourn, and a time to dance;

A time to throw away stones, and a time to gather stones
   together;
A time to embrace, and a time to refrain from
   embracing;
A time to seek, and a time to lose;
A time to keep, and a time to throw away;
A time to tear, and a time to sew;
A time to keep silence, and a time to speak;
A time to love, and a time to hate;
A time for war, and a time for peace.

Note that, according to Ecclesiastes, *at one time of life you
may be called upon to do exactly the opposite of what another
time would require.* A Plan B that would be perfect at 30
may be all wrong at 60. Age 30 may be your time to plant,
and 60 may call for a time to pluck up what is planted. If
you continue your perfectly good age 30 plan when you're
60, what was once the proper path would become inappropriate and lead you astray.

Finding and living the good life means paying continu-
ous attention to what you need to *sustain* growth in all areas
of life—your physical, vocational, emotional, and spiritual
health and the well-being of those around you. You may
decide to be a workaholic for a short period in order to get
a project off the ground or a certain task done. But beware
if you shortchange your physical and emotional health and
sacrifice family obligations and friendships over a long period of time. A good Plan B—a good life—consists of
meeting more than material needs. It always means satis-

fying your longing for relationships, peace of mind, time to reflect, and room to grow in all your humanness.

All religions seem to recognize that different stages in life call for different solutions. The Hindu religion has a stage called "householder," where it's recognized that the individual will concentrate more on the material things necessary to provide for the family. Later, there's a stage that calls for the balance to be shifted to a more spiritual way of life, after the responsibilities of marriage and parenthood have been met.

Most traditional cultures recognize work, struggle, and the gathering of material goods as the primary task, while weaving a spiritual thread throughout this daily effort. In this way, traditional religions and societies have sanctified the material and laboring aspects of life. But modern culture seems to keep different aspects of life in tightly separate cubicles. In present-day society, the very necessary gathering of material goods has grown out of proportion, crowding out room for any other purpose or meaning.

## LIVING THE GOOD LIFE

Look at the following quiz and see whether your answers are providing you with the ability to live the Good Life:

  _____ 1. Do you have daily, weekly, and monthly time to enjoy the fruits of your labor?

  _____ 2. Is the necessary rush of your life leaving you

with no rest, enjoyment, or appreciation of what you have?

_____ 3. Do you feel an inner calm and peace, in spite of a busy schedule?

_____ 4. Are you following your own true path in life?

_____ 5. Are you your Authentic Self?

_____ 6. Do you know who your Authentic Self should be?

_____ 7. Are your role models ones who incorporate the moral, spiritual, and ethical values you hope to achieve?

_____ 8. Do you live your life superficially, or do you search for deeper meanings in the events you encounter?

_____ 9. Do you make necessary changes to alter your script?

_____ 10. If you died tomorrow, would you be satisfied with the way you've lived your life?

This quiz is probably the most difficult one so far to respond to with "correct" answers. The correct answers to these questions are the result of a lifetime's journey to find the ultimate solution. But it's useful to know what the questions are. When you realize you're short of your goal, you must figure out what will get you to where you want to be and what changes are required to get there. Chapter

Twelve is designed to put into plain terms what will help you find your Ultimate Solution—Living the Good Life.

Rainer Maria Rilke, the German poet, had a lovely concept in his *Letters to a Young Poet*—it was to live the questions, not the answer. The answer is to live the good life. *How to get there* is the question that should occupy your life's journey. If purpose and meaning makes your life worthwhile, then the Ultimate Solution is to find what your purpose and meaning consist of.

Finding the good life means *consciously choosing* among the many options available to you. So often, we let life or chance make the choices for us. It's important to become aware when something doesn't feel right, or when *you* don't feel right. Trust your gut reaction—remember, it's almost never wrong. Then examine your Plan A. As we saw in the examples of Ecclesiastes and the Hindu householder, what's an excellent plan during one period of life can become outmoded, irrelevant, and downright *wrong* during another stage. Don't gather stones when it's time to throw them away.

If Plan A no longer works, Plan B is your golden opportunity to live the good life. Living the good life always means living as your Authentic Self. And finding the purpose and meaning of *your* life means living your own beliefs and values. Though each Authentic Self is unique, because beliefs and values may differ, authentic selves share certain recognizable characteristics. These characteristics are the ones you will develop as you move toward a better life.

What are these characteristics, which are not individual but run as a thread throughout the human race? They are universal truths that all cultures and traditions have valued through the ages. These characteristics are trustworthiness, truthfulness, integrity, generosity, patience, compassion, forgiveness, and love. You must be true to yourself, a person of your word, someone of the highest integrity. You must care patiently for those who are vulnerable, refrain from holding grudges, and most important—and most difficult—shine with love to those around you. Traditional cultures wove these threads, which are spiritual aspects of life, throughout the grit and grime of gathering their daily bread. Our modern culture gets to the bottom line—the daily bread—and all too often forgets what that daily bread is meant to feed—the whole person, not just the material body.

The good life is not owning a Porsche, having millions in the bank, and wearing beautiful clothes and jewelry. Many of us personally know or have read about people who have all of the above who live lives of misery and depression. *The good life consists of doing as well as you can in the material world, taking care of the spiritual aspects of your being, and making a positive difference in the world around you.* Any Plan B you choose that leads to the good life *must* include a plan for the spiritual, nonmaterialistic aspects of being. Otherwise you'll be left, over and over again, with a feeling of emptiness that something is missing in your life.

Lifestyle is a very popular concept. The media openly tries to sell this concept as something that will make you happy. Though lifestyle is very important, and consciously choosing one that suits you should take much time and energy, don't confuse lifestyle with Life. Our culture often confuses the two. Solutions for lifestyles are important because they place you in your proper setting—the right region of the country, the spouse you choose above all others, the career that suits you, the religion or political party that suits your needs. Lifestyle tells you where to put down roots, whether to live more simply, whether to come out if you're gay, how much to become involved in community affairs, whether to marry, and whether to have children. Then once you're in your proper setting, your Authentic Self has room to grow.

But don't confuse lifestyle with Life. When people say that old lament, "Is that all there is?," usually they have the material trappings, but still sense a void within. Lifestyle is the house you build to live in; you furnish the interior with a life, and without it the house feels empty. This emptiness is keenly felt by many people who don't develop the broad moral, ethical, and spiritual values we spoke of, though they may never realize what's lacking. Your Plan B—to find the Ultimate Solution and Live the Good Life—must be a plan that brings depth and meaning to you and eliminates any shallowness and superficiality. *When your life has spiritual depth, you'll no longer have an inner void that leaves you feeling unfulfilled and empty.*

When you're bouncing from relationship to relationship, in the wrong career, or cooped up in the city when you dream of country living, your frustration, misery, and discontent prevents you from developing the more spiritual aspects of yourself—essentially preventing you from becoming your Authentic Self. How can you grow to be more patient, compassionate, forgiving, and loving in these circumstances? If this area of your life has been undeveloped, *you are not a bad person.* Most probably, you've been prevented from Living the Good Life by a lifestyle that needs changing to accommodate your life. You need to reconsider your plan.

Real solutions enable you to live life to the fullest. The Ultimate Solution is to choose a plan that allows your lifestyle and life to coincide in such a way that your material needs are met, your emotional needs are taken care of, and your questions answered as you make your way through life. These answers are explanations of the deep questions people ask—"Why am I here?" "What is the meaning of life?" "Is there a purpose to life or is it all just due to chance?"

Naturally, when you're wrestling with baby's diapers, a full-time job, and unpaid bills, these explorations may seem esoteric at best. But if you don't allow yourself time to be *you*, if you lose yourself in all the busyness, then you'll begin to be depleted and run on empty. Even though in the "householder" stage there's very little time for contemplation, it's essential that you take some time to examine your plan and make sure your lifestyle and your life are on the right track. As long as you *are* on that track, you can go as fast or as slow as you wish. If you're on the wrong track, though, you'll eventually derail and it takes so much time to climb back up again. So it's important, in all your busyness, never to give up on the plan that leads to becoming the self you're meant to be.

Look and listen for the rhythms of your own life— they're your clues as to how to find your Ultimate Solution. Your Plan B to find the good life should always consist of taking care of your own physical, emotional, and spiritual needs while considering the needs of those you're close to.

But as you grow and change, those needs may change also. The little child needs milk and pablum; the adult needs different food. You may need to change your lifestyle, either slightly or drastically, in order to accommodate your interior space—your life—which needs a nurturing place to grow and develop over a long period of time.

So in choosing Plan B at any stage of life, follow all the steps you've encountered in the previous chapters. Look at any problems you may have. Think in terms of solutions to them and find the correct solutions for yourself. Assess your Plan A—can it be modified or restored, or do you need Plan B? Then remember that Plan B consists of getting unstuck, and that you need to take time to *emotionally* get ready to implement your plan. Finally, ask, "What's the Solution?" and research, prioritize, brainstorm, do productive daydreaming and journal keeping, and always ask yourself, "What's the Third Way?"—the way where all parties get their needs met, instead of one person at the expense of the other.

If you follow this system thoughtfully, your plan will encompass every aspect of life and will resolve all the lifestyle issues that prevent you from Living the Good Life. Your physical and emotional needs will be met in a way that brings you calm and purpose. You'll have the space to explore the deep questions of life, whose answers evolve over years and decades and finally, after much struggle, lead to wisdom.

How we live our lives furnishes the shades and nuances that color our dreams. This is easy to see in the example of city versus country living. Living in a large city such as

New York, Boston, Chicago, or Los Angeles provides the constant stimulation of humanity, sights, and events that are essential to people with a certain temperament or in certain professional fields. Country living usually provides a simpler life, less outside stimulation, and more interaction with nature, which appeals to people with different temperaments and needs. Usually, the differing experiences lead to different patterns of thinking and acting. The city dweller has more exterior experiences, while the country dweller has more opportunity for interior ones. If they wish, city dwellers have stimulation at any time of the day or night. Country dwellers live by the pattern of seasons— busy times and quiet times. This analogy shows why all the lifestyle issues are so important—each one influences not only how you *live* your life, but how you *see* life, how you perceive the world and your place in it.

There are two major reasons for getting stuck and becoming derailed from your journey toward your Ultimate Solution. Either your Plan A was unrealistic or unrealizable and never worked in the first place, or you had a good plan for living life—the plan did work—but now you've reached a different stage, and the old plan is no longer relevant. One of the most common needs for Plan B is that a new stage has been reached and all the goals Plan A strove for have been satisfied. The Plan A of the student will differ from the Plan A of the new parent. And when those plans get off course, different Plan B's are called for. *Living the Good Life means choosing a plan appropriate to your stage of life.* When a plan has worked for a long time, it's easy to get lulled, drift along on inertia, and think your plan is still working when it's not. Remember, if you have a nagging feeling that something's off base, pay attention to it so that you can continue to grow and find your Ultimate Solution.

From time immemorial, philosophers and sages have recognized the need to adapt to different stages of life. The Greek concept of the seven stages of man has been updated to the more modern concept of Gail Sheehy's *Passages*. The child becomes a student and adolescent; the student becomes a worker; the worker adds a home and family and becomes a householder; the householder spends years acquiring and meeting the needs of that family; the children leave; the individual or couple, though still working, have more free time; then comes retirement and a chance for other opportunities and fulfillment; and finally comes old age and eventually death.

The secret to the Ultimate Solution and Living the Good Life is changing your plan as you move through the different stages of life. Sometimes this calls for a change in lifestyle to allow your Authentic Self to continue developing; sometimes it calls for a change in life—a change in your attitudes or values. Remember, allowing your Authentic Self to grow and develop is the opposite of selfishness. Many people confuse the two. Selfishness is paying attention to your own wants at the expense of others, whereas paying attention to your self is focusing on who you were truly meant to be in order to fulfill your life's purpose. If, after careful thought, you're confused by this issue, consider talking it over with a trusted friend or counselor. It's an important topic, and many people remain stuck upon its shoals. Without resolution, you will find it difficult to become your Authentic Self.

What is an Authentic Self? Here's an illustration of a person I saw fleetingly, years ago, and think of as a perfect example: I was waiting for the bus in Manhattan in order to go to a concert at Lincoln Center. One pulled up and I was puzzled to see that everyone was crowded into the rear, while there was only one person up front. I got on and soon saw the reason why. There was a large, psychotic man raving in the front seat, cursing and screaming about "the war," and everyone was afraid and huddling in the back. This being Manhattan, people didn't leave, but just gave him as wide a berth as possible.

I was calculating how long I'd stay on the bus, and when I'd be near enough to leave and walk the rest of the way, when a little old lady got off, not leaving by the rear exit, but walking out through the front door and stopping to take this man's hand, look into his eyes, and softly say, "God bless you." The man immediately quieted down and was calm for the rest of the trip. I'm sure the other passengers shared my shame and guilt for the discrepancy between what this woman had done and what we were prepared—or not prepared—to do. I've never forgotten that moment. It has remained with me to show me what love and compassion can do—the love shown by a little old lady who could have been knocked down by the physical, let alone psychotic, strength of that man.

Crazed as you may feel at the moment with the myriad details of your own existence, you have the capacity either to become the woman in this example, or to at least recognize the fact that she represents true health and anything less falls short. When you get unstuck from the work, family, and relationship problems that keep you ensnared, you have the ability to finally grow into the person you've always wanted to meet—your true self.

We each have a gift to bring to the world. Plan B is your chance to bring that gift to fruition. By implementing your plan and getting unstuck from your problems, you can bring that most precious gift—your Authentic Self—to the world.

# EPILOGUE

The greatest privilege of my career has been to become partners with patients and couples as they change. It's wonderful to see the glow of people who've been "lost" and now are "found." The joy and happiness they feel as they experience the Solution-Oriented Life is the payoff for all their hard labor. This process has been repeated hundreds of times over decades. The purpose of this book has been to impart these principles to you so that you can transform your life from a present difficult existence to the Solution-Oriented Life you were meant to have. I hope this book has accomplished that purpose and that you will reach toward life lived to its fullest.

You should now be able to go forward on this journey we call life and recognize situations that are good for you, alter those that have the potential for *becoming* good, and find Plan B's that help you leave impossible or undesirable circumstances. I hope that reading *Plan B* will help *you* have

that glow—the feeling of finding oneself that so often occurs in the therapist's office. And most of all, I hope you
will find yourself living a Solution-Oriented Life that is
filled with answers to your most difficult problems.

# For Further Reading

Sarah Ban Breathnach. *Something More* (New York: Warner Books, 1998).

Melody Beattie. *Codependent No More* (Center City, Minn.: Hazelden Press, 1996).

Lee Canter and Marlene Canter. *Assertive Discipline for Parents*, revised edition (New York: HarperCollins, 1993).

Peter F. Drucker. *Managing in a Time of Great Change* (New York: Dutton, 1998).

Edward M. Hallowell, M.D. *Worry* (New York: Ballantine Books, 1998).

John S. Hammond, Ralph L. Keeney, and Howard Raiffa. *Smart Choices* (Boston: Harvard Business School Press, 1999).

Frances Hesselbein, Marshall Goldsmith, and Richard Beckhard, editors. *The Organization of the Future* (San Francisco: Jossey-Bass, 1997).

Peter D. Kramer. *Should You Leave?* (New York: Penguin Books, 1999).

Elisabeth Kübler-Ross. *On Death and Dying* (New York: Touchstone, 1997).

Alan Lakein. *How to Get Control of Your Time and Your Life* (New York: New American Library, 1996).

Harriet G. Lerner. *The Dance of Anger* (New York: Harper-Collins, 1997).

Jerilyn Ross. *Triumph over Fear* (New York: Bantam Books, 1995).

Sidney B. Simon and Suzanne Simon. *Forgiveness* (New York: Warner Books, 1991).

Douglas Stone, Bruce Patton, and Sheila Heen. *Difficult Conversations* (New York: Viking Penguin, 1999).

Deborah Tannen, Ph.D. *You Just Don't Understand* (New York: Ballantine Books, 1991).

# INDEX

Love and relationships, 129
Loyalty, changes in, 186

Major depression, 205
Mastering circumstances, 49
Matching Plan As
    and depression, 215
    for relationships, 131
    and solution, finding, 39–40, 42
Materialism, 269, 272, 273
Meaning in life. *See* Purpose and
    meaning in life, finding
Meltdowns of Plan A
    depression from, 209
    and extraordinary circumstances,
        255
    and solution, finding, 34–35, 39–40,
        43, 47, 51, 52
    unstuck, getting, 74
Message to yourself, 145
Modified Dreams, 34, 47, 52, 208–9
Mourning
    dreams, lost, 88–89
    loss, 209, 252, 265
"Musts," 232, 242

Need(s)
    for change, realizing, 66, 68–74, 93
    fulfilling, 102
    life stages and, 267–68
    for perfection, 234–35, 236, 238
    of safety and security, 225, 239
    and unstuck, getting, 56–68
Negativity and depression, 210
Negotiations and power, 150–51
Neurosis, recognizing, 193–94
"Never" statements, avoiding, 136

Obsession, 227–28
One step at a time, 37–38, 82
Options, 16–17, 81–82, 102, 271
"Oughts," 232–33, 242

Pain of problems, 3, 9–10, 13, 96
*Passages* (Sheehy), 277
Past experiences
    depression from, 209–16, 220–21
    and unstuck, getting, 58, 63–65
Patterns

breaking, 146–49
    depression from, 215–23
    giving up, 140
    synergetic effects of abusive, 218–
        19
Perfection, need for, 234–35, 236,
    238
Plan A (original scenario)
    Broken Dreams, 34, 42–43, 47, 52,
        209
    as cause of problem, 9, 14–15, 17,
        21, 23, 29
    defined, 4–5
    fantasies, 44, 47, 50, 91, 222–23
    Modified Dreams, 34, 47, 52, 208–
        9
    Unsullied Dreams, 34, 38, 208
    work scenarios, 182–83
    *See also* Matching Plan As;
        Meltdowns of Plan A; Solution,
        finding
Plan B. *See* Solution-Oriented Life
Postpartum depression, 206–7
Power in relationships, 149–54
Powerless, feeling, 131–32, 145, 146,
    148–49, 203
Prioritizing method, 82–84
Proactiveness of work career, 186–88,
    193, 196
Problem assessment
    alternatives, 3, 6, 16, 17, 26–27
    consequences of solutions, 28
    defined, 3
    denial, 16
    energy wasted by problems, 10–11,
        *11*, 122–23
    fear of healthy change, 17–18
    living the correct life, 12–13
    pain of problems, 3, 9–10, 13, 96
    Plan A as cause, 9, 14–15, 17, 21,
        23, 29
    problems out of your control,
        resolving, 172–79
    psychotherapy, 10
    realizing you have a problem, 11–
        19
    safe to discover options, 16–17
    solution, finding, 24–29
    Solution-Oriented Life, 11–29

# ABOUT THE AUTHOR

Stephanie Asker, LCSW, is a licensed clinical social worker who has been in practice for twenty-five years. She received her undergraduate degree in psychology from Barnard College and her master's degree in social work from New York University. She has been licensed in four states: New Jersey, New York, Maryland, and Florida. Her practice has ranged from Main Street to Wall Street, where she founded and was the director of Wall Street Counseling Center.

She has been listed in *Who's Who in the East* and *Who's Who of American Women* and has been quoted in such magazines as *Redbook*, *Family Circle*, and *Good Housekeeping*. She has appeared on cable TV, has done an audio tape for the Behavioral Sciences Tape Library titled "Psychotherapy and the Woman's Movement," has been published in the social work journal *Psychotherapy and the Social Worker*, and has been in demand as a speaker at corporate and civic gatherings. Over the years, she has helped people find solutions to problems by holding seminars and workshops, many on communication skills, on Wall Street as well as for AT&T training courses, Associated Press Bureau chiefs and their wives, Banker's Trust, Continental Insurance, and other organizations.

Before Ms. Asker ever thought of writing this book, she was unwittingly doing research on it. As a psychotherapist and marriage counselor, her practice has always been fairly evenly divided between neuroses (depression, anxiety, panic attacks, and dependency) and marriage and relationship counseling. Whether she was treating blue-collar workers, or middle managers in the suburbs, or CEOs on Wall Street, the problems she encountered were the same: People get stuck and don't know how to get out of the muck surrounding them.

Ms. Asker has had personal experience with many issues dealt with in this book, meeting her future husband at 15, marrying at 18, and giving up a scholarship and dropping out of college when she was expecting their first child. After reading *The Feminine Mystique*, she recognized that she too suffered from The Problem That Has No Name and despite having three young children, returned to school, earned her degrees, and went on to a successful practice. Divorced after twenty-one years, then a single professional woman in Manhattan and since remarried, Ms. Asker and her husband, Jim, now live in Palm Beach County, Florida, where she is in private practice. Her own life experiences have helped her understand the problems of the patients she has worked with and the people who will read this book. Thus, she knows the need for a Solution-Oriented Life, both as a woman and as an experienced psychotherapist.